The Stranger in France; or, A Tour From Devonshire to Paris

Sir John Carr

ESPRIOS DIGITAL PUBLISHING

THE

STRANGER IN FRANCE:

OR,

A TOUR FROM DEVONSHIRE TO PARIS.

ILLUSTRATED BY

ENGRAVINGS IN AQUA TINTA

OF

SKETCHES, TAKEN ON THE SPOT,

BY

JOHN CARR, Esq.

1803.

PREFACE.

The little tour which gave birth to the following remarks, was taken immediately after the exchange of the ratifications of a peace, necessary, but not inglorious to my country, after a contest unexampled in its cause, calamity, extension, vicissitudes and glory; amidst a people who, under the influence of a political change, hitherto unparallelled, were to be approached as an order of beings, exhibiting a moral and political form before but little known to themselves and to the world, in the abrupt removal of habits and sentiments which had silently and uninterruptedly taken deep root in the soil of ages.

During a separation of ten years, we have received very little account of this extraordinary people, which could be relied upon. Dissimilar sensations, excited by their principles and proceedings, ever partially and irregularly known, have depicted unaccording representations of them, and, in the sequel, have exhibited rather a high-coloured, fanciful delineation, than a plain and faithful resemblance of the original. Many are the persons who have been thus misled.

These fugitive sketches, in which an attempt is made to delineate, just as they occurred, those scenes which, to *my* mind at least, were new and interesting, were originally penned for the private perusal of those whom I esteem; and by their persuasion they are now offered to the public eye. Amongst them I must be permitted to indulge in the pride and pleasure of enumerating William Hayley, esq. a name familiar and dear to every elegant and polished mind. Enlightened by his emendations, and supported by the cherishing spirit of his approval, I approach, with a more subdued apprehension, the tribunal of public opinion; and to my friends I dedicate this humble result of a short relaxation from the duties of an anxious and laborious profession. If, by submitting to their wishes, I have erred, I have only to offer, that it is my first, and shall be my last offence.

Totnes, August, 1802. JOHN CARR.

The engravings which accompany this work, are of sketches made on the spot by an untutored pencil, and are introduced for the purpose of illustration only.

CONTENTS.

CHAPTER I.

Torr Abbey.—Cap of Liberty.—Anecdote of English Prejudice.—Fire Ships.—Southampton River.—Netley Abbey.

CHAPTER II.

French Emigrants.—Scene on the Quay of Southampton.—Sail for Havre.—Aged French Priest.—Their respectable Conduct in England.— Their Gratitude.—Make the Port of Havre.—Panic of the Emigrants.— Landing described.—Hôtel de la Paix.—Breakfast Knife.—Municipality.

CHAPTER III.

Passports procured.—Coins.—Town of Havre.—Carts.—Citoyen.— Honfleur.—Deserters.—Prefect de Marine.—Ville de Sandwich.—French Farmers.—Sir Sydney Smith.—Catherine de Medicis.—Light Houses.— Rafts.

CHAPTER IV.

Cheap travelling to Paris.—Diligences.—French Postilions.—Spanish Postilions.—Norman Horses.—Bolbec.—Natives of Caux.—Ivetot.— Return of Religion.—Santerre.—Jacobin.—The Mustard-pot.—National Property.

CHAPTER V.

A female french fib.—Military and Civil Procession.—Madame G.—The Review.—Mons. l'Abbé.—Bridge of Boats.—The Quay.—Exchange.— Theatre.—Rouen.—Cathedral.—St. Ouens.—Prince of Waldec.—Maid of Orleans.

CHAPTER VI.

First Consul's Advertisement.—Something ridiculous.—Eggs.—Criminal Military Tribunal.—French Female Confidence.—Town House.—Convent of Jesuits.—Guillotine.—Governor W— —.

CHAPTER VII.

Filial Piety. — St. Catharine's Mount. — Madame Phillope. — General Ruffin's Trumpet. — Generosity. — Love Infectious. — Masons and Gardeners.

CHAPTER VIII.

Early dinner. — Mante. — Frost. — Duke de Sully. — Approach the Capital. — Norman Barrier. — Paris. — Hôtel de Rouen. — Palais Royal.

CHAPTER IX.

French Reception. — Voltaire. — Restaurateur. — Consular Guard. — Music. — Venetian Horses. — Gates of the Palace. — Gardens of the Thuilleries. — Statues. — The faithful Vase. — The Sabine Picture. — Monsieur Perrègaux. — Marquis de Chatelet. — Madame Perrègaux. — Beaux and Belles of Paris.

CHAPTER X.

Large Dogs. — A Plan for becoming quickly acquainted with Paris. — Pantheon. — Tombs of Voltaire and Rousseau. — Politeness of an Emigrant. — The Beauty of France. — Beauty evanescent. — Place de Carousel. — Infernal Machine. — Fouché. — Seine. — Washerwomen. — Fisherwomen. — Baths.

CHAPTER XI.

David. — Place de la Concorde. — L'Église de Madeleine. — Print-shops. — Notre Dame. — Museum or Palace of Arts. — Hall of Statues. — Laocoon. — Belvidere Apollo. — Socrates.

CHAPTER XII.

Bonaparte. — Artillery. — Mr. Pitt. — Newspapers. — Archbishop of Paris. — Consular Colours. — Religion. — Consular Conversion. — Madame Bonaparte. — Consular Modesty. — Separate Beds. — A Country Scene. — Connubial Affection. — Female Bravery.

CHAPTER XIII.

Breakfast.—Warmth of French Expression.—Rustic Eloquence.—Curious Cause assigned for the late extraordinary Frost.—Madame R——.—Paul I.—Tivoli.—Frescati.

CHAPTER XIV.

Convent of blue Nuns.—Duchesse de Biron.—The bloody Key.—Courts of Justice.—Public Library.—Gobelines.—Miss Linwood.—Garden of Plants.—French Accommodation.—Boot Cleaners.—Cat and Dog Shearers.—Monsieur S—— and Family.

CHAPTER XV.

Civility of a Sentinel.—The Hall of the Legislative Assembly.—British House of Commons.—Captain Bergeret.—The Temple.—Sir Sydney Smith's Escape.—Colonel Phillipeaux.

CHAPTER XVI.

A fashionable Poem.—Frere Rickart.—Religion.—Hôtel des Invalides.— Hall of Victory.—Enemies' Colours.—Sulky Appearance of an English Jack and Ensign.—Indecorum.—The aged Captain.—Military School.—Champ de Mars.—The Garden of Mousseaux.

CHAPTER XVII.

Curious Method of raising Hay.—Lucien Bonaparte's Hôtel.—Opera.— Consular Box.—Madame Bonaparte's Box.—Feydeau Theatre.—Belle Vue.—Versailles.—The Palace of the Petit Trianon.—The Grounds.

CHAPTER XVIII.

Bonaparte's Talents in Finance.—Garrick and the Madman.—Palace of the Conservative Senate.—Process of transferring Oil Paintings from Wood to Canvas.—The Dinner Knife.—Commodities.—Hall of the National Convention.—The Minister Talleyrand's Levee.

CHAPTER XIX.

The College of the Deaf and Dumb.—Abbé Sicard.—Bagatelle.—Police.— Grand National Library.—Bonaparte's Review.—Tambour Major of the Consular Regiment.—Restoration of Artillery Colours.

CHAPTER XX.

Abbè Sieyes.—Consular Procession to the Council Chamber.—10th of August, 1792.—Celerity of Mons. Fouche's Information.—The two Lovers.—Cabinet of Mons. le Grand.—Self-prescribing Physician.—Bust of Robespierre.—His Lodgings.—Corn Hall.—Museum of French Monuments.—Revolutionary Agent.—Lovers of married Women.

CHAPTER XXI.

Picturesque and Mechanical Theatre.—Filtrating and purifying Vases.—English Jacobins.—A Farewell.—Messagerie.—MalMaison.—Forest of Evreux.—Lower Normandy.—Caen.—Hon. T. Erskine.—A Ball.—The Keeper of the Sachristy of Notre Dame.—The two blind Beggars.—Ennui.—St. Lo.—Cherbourg.—England.

GENERAL REMARKS.

Torr Abbey

CHAPTER I.

Torr Abbey. — Cap of Liberty. — Anecdote of English Prejudice. — Fire Ships. — Southampton River. — Netley Abbey.

It was a circumstance, which will be memorable with me, as long as I live, and pleasant to my feelings, as often as I recur to it, that part of my intended excursion to the Continent was performed in the last ship of war, which, after the formal confirmations of the peace, remained, of that vast naval armament, which, from the heights of Torbay, for so many years, presented to the astonished and admiring eye, a spectacle at once of picturesque beauty, and national glory. It was the last attendant in the train of retiring war.

Under the charming roof of Torr Abbey, the residence of George Cary, esq., I passed a few days, until the Megæra was ready to sail for Portsmouth, to be paid off, the commander of which, captain Newhouse, very politely offered to convey my companion, captain W. Cary, and myself, to that port.

In this beautiful spot, the gallant heroes of our navy have often found the severe and perilous duties of the boisterous element alleviated by attentions, which, in their splendid and cordial display, united an elegant taste to a noble spirit of hospitality.

In the Harleian Tracts there is a short, but rather curious account preserved of the sensation produced at the Abbey on the 5th of November, 1688, after the prince of Orange had entered the bay with his fleet, on their passage to Brixham, where he landed: —

"The prince commanded captain M—— to search the lady Cary's house, at Torr Abbey, for arms and horses. The lady entertaining them civilly, said her husband was gone to Plymouth: they brought from thence some horses, and a few arms, but gave no further disturbance to the lady or her house."

Throughout this embarrassing interview, the lady Cary appears to have conducted herself with great temper, dignity and resolution, whilst, on the other hand, the chaplain of that day, whose opinions were not very favourable to the revolution, unlike his present amiable and enlightened successor[1], left his lady in the midst of her perplexities, and fled.

In the Abbey, I was much pleased with an interesting, though not very ornamental trophy of the glorious victory of Aboukir. The truckle heads of the masts of the Aquilon, a french ship of the line, which struck to the brave captain Louis, in that ever memorable battle, were covered with the bonnet rouge; one of these caps of liberty, surmounted with the british flag, has been committed to the care of the family, by that heroic commander, and now constitutes a temporary ornament of their dining-room.

Here we laid in provision for our little voyage, without, however, feeling the same apprehension, which agitated the mind of a fair damsel, in the service of a lady of rank who formerly resided in my neighbourhood, who, preparing to attend her mistress to the Continent, and having heard from the jolly historians of the kitchen, that the food in France was chiefly supplied by the croaking inhabitants of the green and standing pool, contrived, very carefully, to carry over a piece of homebred pork, concealed in her workbag.

Early in the morning after we set sail, we passed through the Needles, which saved us a very considerable circuitous sail round the southern side of the Isle of Wight, a passage which the late admiral Macbride first successfully attempted, for vessels of war, in a ship of the line.

The vessel, in which we sailed, was a fireship; a costly instrument of destruction, which has never been applied during the recent war, and only once, and that unsuccessfully, during the preceding one. We had several of them in commission, although they are confessedly of little utility in these times, and from the immense stores of combustibles with which they are charged, threaten only peril to the commander and his crew.

We soon after dropped anchor, and proceeded to Portsmouth, in search of a packet for Havre-de-Grace. In the street, our trunks were seized by the custom-house officers, whilst conveying to the inn, but after presenting our keys, and requesting immediate search and restoration, they were returned to us without further annoyance. Finding that the masters of the french packets were undetermined when they should sail, we resolved upon immediately leaving this celebrated seaport, and proceeding by water to Southampton, distant about twenty-four miles; where, after a very unpleasant passage, from its blowing with considerable violence soon after we left Portsmouth, we arrived, in a little wherry, about twelve o'clock at night, at the Vine inn, which is very conveniently situated for passengers by the packets.

It will not be required of me, to attempt a minute description of the Southampton river, at a time when I expected, with some reason, as I afterwards understood, to sink to the bottom of it. An observation very natural to persons in our situation occurred to me all the way, viz. that the shores seemed to be too far distant from each other, and that had there been less water, the scenery would have been more delightful; an observation which, however, the next day confirmed, when it presented the safe and tranquil appearance of a mirror.

Southampton.

Finding that the packet for France was not likely to sail immediately, we hired a boat, and proceeded down the river, to view the beautiful ruins of Netley Abbey, in the great court of which we dined, under the shade of aged limes, and amidst the flappings of its feathered and restless tenantry.

As I am no great admirer of tedious details, I shall not attempt an antiquarian history of this delightful spot. I shall leave it to more circumstantial travellers, to enumerate the genealogies of the worthies who occupied it at various eras, and to relate, like a monumental entablature, when, where, and how they lived and died; it will be sufficient to observe, that the site of this romantic abode was granted by Henry VIII, in 1757, to a sir William Paulet, and that after having had many merry monks for its masters, who, no doubt, performed their matutinæ laudes and nocturnæ vigiliæ with devout exactness; that it is at length in the possession of Mr. Dance, who has a very fine and picturesque estate on that side of the river, of which these elegant ruins constitute the chief ornament. The church still exhibits a beautiful specimen of gothic architecture, but its tottering remains will rapidly share the fate of the neighbouring pile, which time has prostrated on the earth, and covered with his thickest shade of ivy.

Our watermen gave us a curious description of this place, and amused us not a little with their ridiculous anacronisms.

"I tell you what," said one of them, contradicting the other, "you are in the wrong, Bob, indeed you are wrong, don't mislead them gentlemen, that there Abbey is in the true roman style, and was built by a man they call— —, but that's neither here nor there, I forget the name, however, its a fine place, and universally allowed to be very old. I frequently rows gentlefolks there, and picks up a great deal about it."

On our return the tide was at its height, the sun was setting in great glory, the sky and water seemed blended in each other, the same red rich tint reigned throughout, the vessels at anchor appeared suspended in the air, the spires of the churches were tipped with the golden ray; a scene of more beauty, richness, and tranquillity I never beheld.

NOTES:

[1] Rev. John Halford.

CHAPTER II.

French Emigrants. — Scene on the Quay of Southampton. — Sail for Havre. — Aged French Priest. — Their respectable Conduct in England. — Their Gratitude. — Make the Port of Havre. — Panic of the Emigrants. — Landing described. — Hotel de la Paix. — Breakfast Knife. — Municipality.

During the whole of the second day after our arrival, the town of Southampton was in a bustle, occasioned by the flocking in of a great number of french emigrants, who were returning to their own country, in consequence of a mild decree, which had been passed in their favour. The scene was truly interesting, and the sentiment which it excited, delightful to the heart.

A respectable curé, who dined in the same room with us at our inn, was observed to eat very little; upon being pressed to enlarge his meal, this amiable man said, with tears starting in his eyes, "Alas! I have no appetite; a very short time will bring me amongst the scenes of my nativity, my youth, and my happiness, from which a remorseless revolution has parted me for these ten long years; I shall ask for those who are dear to me, and find them for ever gone. Those who are left will fill my mind with the most afflicting descriptions; no, no, I cannot eat, my good sir."

About noon, they had deposited their baggage upon the quay, which formed a pile of aged portmanteaus, and battered trunks. Parties remained to protect them, previous to their embarkation. The sun was intensely hot, they were seated under the shade of old umbrellas, which looked as if they had been the companions of their banishment.

Their countenances appeared strongly marked with the pious character of resignation, over which were to be seen a sweetness, and corrected animation, which seemed to depict at once the soul's delight, of returning to its native home, planted wherever it may be, and the regret of leaving a nation, which, in the hour of flight and misery, had nobly enrolled them in the list of her own children, and had covered them with protection.

To the eternal honour of these unhappy, but excellent people, be it said, that they have proved themselves worthy of being received in such a sanctuary. Our country has enjoyed the benefit of their unblemished morals, and their mild, polite, and unassuming manners, and wherever destiny has placed them, they have industriously relieved the national burden of their support by diffusing the knowledge of a language, which good sense, and common interest, should long since have considered as a valuable branch of education.

To those of my friends, who exercise the sacred functions of religion, as established in this country, I need not offer an apology, for paying an humble tribute of common justice to these good, and persecuted men; who, from habit, pursue a mode of worship, a little differing in form, but terminating in the same great and glorious centre. The enlightened liberality of the british clergy will unite, in paying that homage to them, which they, in my presence, have often with enthusiasm, and rapture, offered up to the purity, and sanctity of their characters. Many of them informed me, that they had received the most serviceable favours from our clergy, administered with equal delicacy, and munificence.

Amongst these groups were some females, the wives and daughters of toulonese merchants, who left their city when lord Hood abandoned that port. The politeness and attention, which were paid to them by the men, were truly pleasing. It was the good breeding of elegant habits, retaining all their softness in the midst of adversity, sweetened with the sympathy of mutual and similar sufferings.

They had finished their dinner, and were drinking their favourite beverage of coffee. Poor wanderers! the water was scarcely turned brown with the few grains which remained of what they had purchased for their journey.

I addressed them, by telling them, that I had the happiness of being a passenger with them, in the same vessel; they said they were fortunate to have in their company one of that nation, which would be dear to them as long as they lived. A genteel middle aged woman offered to open a little parcel of fresh coffee, which they had purchased in the town for the voyage, and begged to make some for me. By her manner, she seemed to wish me to consider it, more as the humble offering of gratitude, than of politeness, or perhaps both were blended in the offer. In the afternoon, their baggage was searched by the revenue officers, who, on this occasion, exercised a liberal gentleness, which gave but little trouble, and no pain. They who brought nothing into a country but the recollection of their miseries, were not very likely to carry much out of it, but the remembrance of its generosity.

At seven o'clock in the evening we were all on board, and sailed with a gentle breeze down the river: we carried with us a good stock of vegetables, which we procured fresh, from the admirable market of Southampton. Upon going down into the cabin, I was struck, and at first shocked, with seeing a very aged man, stretched at his length upon pillows and clothes, placed on the floor, attended by two clergymen, and some women, who, in their attentions to this apparently dying old gentleman, seemed to have forgotten their own comfortless situation, arising from so many persons being crowded in so small a space, for our numbers above and below amounted to sixty. Upon inquiry, they informed me, that the person whose appearance had so affected me, had been a clergyman of great repute and esteem at Havre, that he was then past the age of ninety five years, scarcely expected to survive our short voyage, but was anxious to breathe his last in his own country. They spoke of him, as a man who in other times, and in the fulness of his faculties, had often from his pulpit, struck with terror and contrition, the trembling souls of his auditors, by the force of his exalted eloquence; who had embellished the society in which he moved, with his elegant attainments; and who had relieved the unhappy, with an enlarged heart and munificent hand—A mere mass of misery, and helpless infirmities, remained of all these noble qualities!

During the early part of the night, we made but little way—behind, the dark shadowy line of land faded in mist; before us, the moon spread a stream of silver light upon the sea. The soft stillness of this repose of nature was broken only by the rippling of the light wave against the head and sides of the vessel, and by the whistling of the helmsman, who, with the helm between his knees, and his arms crossed, alternately watching the compass and the sail, thus invoked the presence of the favouring breeze.

Leaving him, and some few of our unfortunate comrades, to whom the motion of the sea was more novel than gratifying, we descended into the steerage, (for our births in the cabin were completely occupied by females). As we were going down the ladder, the appearance of so many recumbent persons, faintly distinguishable by the light of a solitary taper, reminded us of a floating catacomb; here, crawling under a cot which contained two very corpulent priests, upon a spare cable, wrapt up in our own great coats, we resigned ourselves to rest.

The next day, without having made much progress in our little voyage, we arose, and assembled round the companion, which formed our breakfast table; at dinner, we were enabled to spread a handsome table of refreshments, to which we invited all our fellow passengers who were capable of partaking of them, many of whom were preparing to take their scanty meal, removed from us at the head of the vessel. For this little act of common civility, we were afterwards abundantly repaid, by the thankfulness of all, and the serviceable attentions of some of our charming guests, when we landed; an instance of which I shall afterwards have occasion to mention. The wind slackened during the day, but in the evening it blew rather fresh, and about nine o'clock the next morning, after a night passed something in the same way as the former, we were awakened being informed that we were within in a league of Havre; news by no means disagreeable, after the dead dulness of a sea calm.

The appearance of the coast was high, rugged, and rocky; to use a good marine expression, it looked ironbound all along shore. To the east, upon an elevated point of land, are two noble light houses, of very beautiful construction, which I shall have occasion to describe hereafter.

At some little distance, we saw considerable flights of wild ducks. The town and bason lie round the high western point from the lights, below which there is a fine pebbled beach. The quays are to the right and left within the pier, upon the latter of which there is a small round tower. It was not the intention of our packet captain to go within the pier, for the purpose of saving the port-anchorage dues, which amount to eight pounds sterling, but a government boat came off, and ordered the vessel to hawl close up to the quay, an order which was given in rather a peremptory manner. Upon our turning the pier, we saw as we warped up to the quay, an immense motley crowd, flocking down to view us. A panic ran throughout our poor fellow passengers. From the noise and confusion on shore, they expected that some recent revolution had occurred, and that they were upon the point of experiencing all the calamities, which they had before fled from; they looked pale and agitated upon each other, like a timid and terrified flock of sheep, when suddenly approached by their natural enemy the wolf. It turned out, however, that mere curiosity, excited by the display of english colours, had assembled this formidable rabble, and that the order which we received from the government boat, was given for the purpose of compelling the captain to incur, and consequently to pay, the anchorage dues. In a moment we were beset by a parcel of men and boys, half naked, and in wooden shoes, who hallooing and "sacre dieuing" each other most unmercifully, began, without further ceremony, to seize upon every trunk within their reach, which they threw into their boats lying alongside.

By a well-timed rap upon the knuckles of one of these marine functionaries, we prevented our luggage from sharing the same fate. It turned out, that there was a competition for carrying our trunks on shore, for the sake of an immoderate premium, which they expected to receive, and which occasioned our being assailed in this violent manner. Our fellow-passengers were obliged to go on shore with these vociferous watermen, who had the impudence and inhumanity to charge them two livres each, for conveying them to the landing steps, a short distance of about fifty yards. Upon their landing, we were much pleased to observe that the people offered them neither violence nor insult. They were received with a sullen silence, and a lane was made for them to pass into the town. The poor old clergyman who had survived the passage, was left on board, in the care of two benevolent persons, until he could be safely and comfortably conveyed on shore. We soon afterwards followed our fellow-passengers in the captain's boat, by which plan we afforded these extortioners a piece of salutary information, very necessary to be made known to them, that although we were english, we were not to be imposed upon. I could not help thinking it rather unworthy of our neighbours to exact from us such heavy port dues, when our own demands of a similar nature, are so very trifling. For such an impost, a vessel of the republic, upon its arrival in any of the english ports, would only pay a few shillings. Perhaps this difference will be equalized in some shape, by the impending commercial treaty, otherwise, a considerable partial advantage will accrue to the french from their passage packets. Upon our landing, and entering the streets, I was a little struck with the appearance of the women, who were habited in a coarse red camlet jacket, with a high apron before, long flying lappets to their caps, and were mounted upon large heavy wooden shoes, upon each of which a worsted tuft was fixed, in rude imitation of a rose. The appearance and clatter of these sabots, as they are called, leave upon the mind an impression of extreme poverty and wretchedness.

They are, however, more favoured than the lower order of females in Scotland. Upon a brisk sprightly chamber-maid entering my room one day at an inn in Glasgow, I heard a sound which resembled the pattering of some web-footed bird, when in the act of climbing up the miry side of a pond. I looked down upon the feet of this bonny lassie, and found that their only covering was procured from the mud of the high street—adieu! to the tender eulogies of the pastoral reed! I have never thought of a shepherdess since with pleasure.

I could not help observing the ease, dexterity, and swiftness, with which a single man conveyed all our luggage, which was very heavy, to the custom-house, and afterwards to the inn, in a wheelbarrow, which differed from ours, only in being larger, and having two elastic handles of about nine feet long. At the custom-house, notwithstanding what the english papers have said of the conduct observed here, we were very civilly treated, our boxes were only just opened, and some of our packages were not examined at all. Away we had them whirled, to the Hôtel de la Paix, the front of which looks upon the wet-dock, and is embellished with a large board, upon which is recorded, in yellow characters, as usual, the superior advantages of this house over every other hôtel in Havre. Upon our arrival, we were ushered up a large dirty staircase into a lofty room, upon the first floor, all the windows of which were open, divided, as they always are in France, in the middle, like folding doors; the floor was tiled, a deal table, some common rush chairs, two very fine pier glasses, and chandeliers to correspond, composed our motley furniture. I found it to be a good specimen of french inns, in general. We were followed by our hostess, the porter, two cooks, with caps on their heads, which had once been white, and large knives in their hands, who were succeeded by two chamber-maids, all looking in the greatest hurry and confusion, and all talking together, with a velocity, and vehemence, which rendered the faculty of hearing almost a misfortune. They appeared highly delighted to see us, talked of our dress, sir Sidney Smith, the blockade, the noble english, the peace, and a train of etceteras. At length we obtained a little cessation, of which we immediately seized the advantage, by directing them to show us to our bedrooms, to procure abundance of water hot and cold, to get us a good breakfast as soon as possible, and to prepare a good dinner for us at four o'clock. Amidst a peal of tongues, this clamorous procession retired.

After we had performed our necessary ablutions, and had enjoyed the luxury of fresh linen, we sat down to some excellent coffee, accompanied with boiled milk, long, delicious rolls, and tolerably good butter, but found no knives upon the table; which, by the by, every traveller in France is presumed to carry with him: having mislaid my own, I requested the maid to bring me one. The person of this damsel, would certainly have suffered by a comparison with those fragrant flowers, to which young poets resemble their beloved mistresses; as soon as I had preferred my prayer, she very deliberately drew from her pocket a large clasp knife, which, after she had wiped on her apron, she presented to me, with a "voila monsieur." I received this dainty present, with every mark of due obligation, accompanied, at the same time, with a resolution not to use it, particularly as my companions (for we had two other english gentlemen with us) had directed her to bring some others to them. This delicate instrument was as savoury as its mistress, amongst the various fragrancies which it emitted, garlic seemed to have the mastery.

About twelve o'clock we went to the hall of the municipality, to procure our passports for the interior, and found it crowded with people upon the same errand. We made our way through them into a very handsome antiroom, and thence, by a little further perseverance, into an inner room, where the mayor and his officers were seated at a large table covered with green cloth. To show what reliance is to be placed upon the communications of english newspapers, I shall mention the following circumstance: my companion had left England, without a passport, owing to the repeated assurances of both the ministerial and opposition prints, and also of a person high in administration, that none were necessary.

The first question propounded to us by the secretary was, "citizens, where are your passports?" I had furnished myself with one; but upon hearing this question, I was determined not to produce it, from an apprehension that I should cover my friend, who had none, with suspicion, so we answered, that in England they were not required of frenchmen, and that we had left our country with official assurances that they would not be demanded of us here.

They replied to us, by reading a decree, which rigorously required them of foreigners, entering upon the territories of the republic, and they assured us, that this regulation was at that moment reciprocal with every other power, and with England in particular. The decree of course closed the argument. We next addressed ourselves to their politeness (forgetting that the revolution had made sad inroads upon it) and requested them, as we had been misled, and had no other views of visiting the country, but those of pleasure, and improvement, that they would be pleased to grant us our passports for the interior. To this address, these high authorities, who seemed not much given to "the melting mood," after making up a physiognomy, as severe, and as *iron bound* as their coast, laconically observed, that the laws of the republic must be enforced, that they should write to our embassador to know who we were, and that in the mean time they would make out our passports for the town, the barriers of which we were not to pass. Accordingly, a little fat gentleman, in a black coat, filled up these official instruments, which were copied into their books, and both signed by us; he then commenced our "signalement," which is a regular descriptive portrait of the head of the person who has thus the honour of sitting to the municipal portrait painters of the département de la Seine inferieure.

This portrait is intended, as will be immediately anticipated, to afford encreased facilities to all national guards, maréchaussées, thief takers, &c. for placing in "durance vile" the unfortunate original, should he violate the laws.

The signalement is added in the margin, to the passport, and also registered in the municipal records, which, from their size, appeared to contain a greater number of heads and faces, thus depicted, than any museum or gallery I ever beheld.

How correct the likenesses in general are, I leave to the judgment of others, after I have informed them, that the hazle eyes of my friend were described "yeux bleus" in this masterly delineation.

If the dead march in Saul had been playing before us all the way, we could not have marched more gravely, or rather sulkily, to our inn. Before us, we had the heavy prospect of spending about ten days in this town, not very celebrated for either beauty, or cleanliness, until the municipality could receive an account of us, from our embassador, who knew no more of us than they did. The other english gentlemen were in the same predicament.

However we determined to pursue the old adage, that what is without remedy, should be without regret, and, english like, grew very merry over a good dinner, consisting of soups, and meat, and fowls, and fish, and vegetables (for such is the order of a french dinner) confectionary and a desert, accompanied with good Burgundy, and excellent Champaign. Our misfortunes must plead our excuse, if the dinner is considered extravagant. Uncle Toby went to sleep when he was unhappy; we solicited consolation in another way. Our signalements afforded us much diversion, which at length was a little augmented by a plan which I mentioned, as likely to furnish us with the means of our liberation. After dinner I waited upon a young gentleman who was under the care of a very respectable merchant, to whom I had the good fortune to have letters of introduction. Through his means I was introduced to Mons. de la M——, who received me with great politeness. In the hurry and occupations of very extensive commercial pursuits, this amiable old gentleman had found leisure to indulge himself in works of taste. His noble fortune enabled him to gratify his liberal inclinations. I found him seated in his compting-house, which, from its handsome furniture and valuable paintings, resembled an elegant cabinet. I stated the conduct of the municipality towards us, and requested his assistance. After he had shown me his apartments, a fine collection of drawings, by some of the first masters, and some more excellent paintings, we parted, with an assurance that he would immediately wait upon the mayor, who was his friend, and had no doubt but that he should in the course of the next day enable us to leave Havre when and in what manner we pleased. With this agreeable piece of intelligence, I immediately returned to the inn, where it induced us to drink health and success to the friendly merchant in another bottle of champaign.

CHAPTER III.

Passports procured. — Coins. — Town of Havre. — Carts. — Citoyen. —
Honfleur. — Deserters. — Prefect de Marine. — Ville de Sandwich. — French
Farmers. — Sir Sydney Smith. — Catherine de Medicis. — Light Houses. —
Rafts.

If Havre had been a Paradise, the feelings of restraint would have discoloured the magic scenery, and turned the green to one barren brown.

As we could relish nothing, until we had procured our release, the first place we visited the next morning was, once more, the residence of the municipality, where we found that our worthy friend had previously arranged every thing to our wishes, and upon his signing a certificate, that we were peaceable citizens, and had no intention to overturn the republic, our passports were made out, and upon an exchange of a little snuff, and a few bows, we retired. The other two englishmen had their wishes gratified, by the same lucky incident, which had assisted us. Having changed our guineas for french money, and as in future, when money is mentioned, it will be in the currency of the country, it perhaps may not be unacceptable to subjoin a table of the old, and new, and republican coins. For every guinea of full weight, which we carried over, we received twenty-four livres, or a louis d'or, which is equal to twenty shillings sterling, of course we lost one shilling upon every good guinea, and more, according to the deficiency of weight. The course of exchange and commission, with our country, I afterwards found at Paris, to be one shilling and eight pence, in the pound sterling, against us, but the difference will be progressively nearer par, as the accustomed relations of commerce resume their former habits. I was surprised to find the ancient monarchical coin in chief circulation, and that of the republic, very confined. Scarce a pecuniary transaction can occur, but the silent, and eloquent medallion of the unhappy monarch, seems to remind these bewildered people of *his* fate, and *their* past misfortunes. Although the country is poor, all their payments are made in cash, this is owing to the shock given by the revolution, to individual, and consequently to paper credit.

To comprehend their money, it must be known, although the french always calculate by livres, as we do by pounds sterling, that the livre is no coin, but computation.

MONARCHICAL COINS.

GOLD.

	s.	d.	
A louis d'or is twenty four livres french, or	20	0	English.

SILVER.

	s.	d.
A grand ecu, or six livre piece,	5	0
An ecu, or three livre piece,	2	6
The vingt quatre sols piece,	1	0
A douze sols piece is twelve pence french, or	0	6
A six sols piece is 6d french, or	0	3

COPPER MIXED WITH SILVER.

A deux sols, or two pence french, and one penny english, is nearly the size of our sixpence, but is copper, with a white or silverish mixture, twelve of these make a vingt quatre sols piece, or one shilling english.

They have also another small piece of nearly the same size and colour, but not so white, and rather thinner, which is one sol and a half, three halfpence french, or three farthings english.

COPPER.

A sol is like our halfpenny, value one penny french, or a halfpenny english, twenty-four of these make an english shilling.

A deux liard piece is half a sol french, or a farthing english.

17

A liard is a farthing french, and of the value of half a farthing english.

NEW COIN.

A thirty sols piece, is a very beautiful and convenient coin, worth one shilling and three pence english, having a good impression of the late king's head on one side, and the goddess of liberty on the other; it was struck in the early part of the revolution.

REPUBLICAN COIN.

SILVER.

A fifteen sols piece is half of the above and very convenient.

COPPER.

A six liard is a bit of copper composition, such as the fine cannon are made of, and is worth three sols french, or a halfpenny, and a farthing english.

A cinq centimes is worth a halfpenny and half a farthing english.

The centimes are of the value of half farthings, five of which are equal to the last coin, they are very small and neat.

An early knowledge of these coins, is very necessary to a stranger, on account of the dishonest advantages which french tradesmen take of their english customers.

To return to my narrative: finding ourselves at liberty to pursue our route, we went from the municipality to the bureau des diligences, and secured our places in the voiture to Rouen, for the next day.

After this necessary arrangement, we proceeded to view the town, which is composed of long and narrow streets. The fronts of the houses, which are lofty, are deformed by the spaces between the naked intersections of the frame work being filled up with mortar, which gives them an appearance of being very heavy, and very mean.

The commerce formerly carried on at Havre, was very extensive. There is here also large manufactories for lace. The theatre is very spacious, well arranged, and as far as we could judge by day-light, handsomely decorated. The players did not perform during our stay. In the vegetable market place, which was much crowded, and large, we saw at this season of the year abundance of fine apples, as fresh in appearance as when they were first plucked from the tree.

In our way there we were accosted by a little ragged beggar boy, who addressed himself to our compassionate dispositions, by the appellation of "très charitable citoyen," but finding we gave nothing, he immediately changed it to "mon chère très charitable monsieur."

The strange uncouth expression of citoyen is generally laid aside, except amongst the immediate officers under government, in their official communications, who, however, renounce it in private, for the more civilized title of "monsieur."

The principal church is a fine handsome building, and had been opened for worship, the Sunday before we arrived: On that day the bell of the Sabbath first sounded, during ten years of revolution, infidelity, and bloodshed!!!

The royal arms are every where removed. They formerly constituted a very beautiful ornament over the door of the hotel of the present prefect, at the head of the market place, but they have been rudely beaten out by battle axes, and replaced by rude republican emblems, which every where (I speak of them as a decoration) seem to disfigure the buildings which bear them. When I made this remark, I must, however, candidly confess, that my mind very cordially accompanied my eye, and that natural sentiment mingled with the observation. The quays, piers, and arsenal are very fine, they, together with the docks, for small ships of war and merchandize, were constructed under the auspices of Lewis XIV, with whom this port was a great favourite.

We saw several groups of men at work in heavy chains. They were soldiers who had offended. They are dressed in *red* jackets and trowsers, which are supposed to increase their disgrace, on account of its being the regimental colour of their old enemy, the english. When my companion, who wore his regimentals, passed them, they all moved their caps to him with great respect.

The town, and consequently the commerce of Rouen, was most successfully blockaded, for near four years, by british commanders, during the late war, and particularly by sir Sidney Smith. It was here, when endeavouring to cut out a vessel, which in point of value, and consideration was unworthy of such an exposure, that this great hero, and distinguished being was made a prisoner of war. The inhabitants, who never speak of him, but with emotions of terror, consider this event as the rash result of a wager conceived over wine. Those who know the character of sir Sidney, will not impute to him such an act of *idle* temerity. No doubt he considered the object, as included in his duty, and it is only to be lamented, that during two lingering years of rigorous, and cruel confinement, in the dungeons of the unhappy sovereign, his country was bereaved of the assistances of her immortal champion, who, in a future season, upon the shores of Acre, so nobly filled up the gloomy chasm of suspended services, by exploits, which to be believed, must not be *adequately* described, and who revenged, by an act of unrivalled glory, the long endurance of sufferings, and indignities hateful to the magnanimous spirit of modern warfare, and unknown to it, until displayed within the walls of a prussian dungeon[2].

I shall hereafter have occasion to mention this extraordinary character, when I speak of his escape from the Temple, the real circumstances attending which are but little known, and which I received from an authority upon which the reader may rely.

This town is not unknown to history. At the celebrated siege of it, in the time of Catharine de Medicis, that execrable princess, distinguished herself by her personal intrepidity. It is said, that she landed here, in a galley, bearing the device of the sun, with these words in greek, "I bring light, and fine weather"—a motto which ill corresponded with her conduct.

With great courage, such as seldom associates with cruel, and ferocious tyrants, she here on horseback, at the head of her army, exposed herself to the fire of the cannon, like the most veteran soldiers, and betrayed no symptoms of fear, although the bullets flew about her in all directions. When desired by the duke of Guise, and the constable de Montmorenci not to expose her person so much, the brave, but sanguinary Catharine replied, "Have I not more to lose than you, and do you think I have not as much courage?"

The walk, through la ville de Sandwiche, to the light houses, which are about two miles from Havre, is very pleasing. The path lay through flax and clover fields. In this part of the country, the farmers practise an excellent plan of rural economy, which is also used in Dorsetshire, and some few other counties, of confining their cattle by a string to a spot of pasture, until they have completely cleared it.

Light-house at Havre

Upon the hill, ascending to the cliffs, are several very elegant chateaus and gardens, belonging to the principal inhabitants of the town.

Monsieur B——, the prefect de marine, has a beautiful residence here. We were accidentally stopping at his gate, which was open, to view the enchanting prospects, which it presented to us, when the polite owner observed us, and with that amiableness, and civility, which still distinguish the descendants of the ancient families of rank in France, of which he is one, requested us to enter, and walked with us round his grounds, which were disposed with great taste. He afterwards conducted us to his elegant house, and gave us dried fruit, and excellent burgundy, after which we walked round the village to the light houses. From him we learnt, that the farmers here, as in England, were very respectable, and had amassed considerable wealth during the war. The approach to the light houses, through a row of elms, is very pleasant; they stand upon an immense high perpendicular cliff, and are lofty square buildings, composed of fine light brown free stone, the entrance is handsome, over which there is a good room, containing four high windows, and a lodging room for the people, who have the care of the light, the glass chamber of which we reached, after ascending to a considerable height, by a curious spiral stone stair case. The lantern is composed, of ninety immense reflecting lamps, which are capable of being raised or depressed with great ease by means of an iron windlass. This large lustre, is surrounded with plates of the thickest french glass, fixed in squares of iron, and discharges a prodigious light, in dark nights. A furnace of coal, was formerly used, but this has been judiciously superseded by the present invention. Round the lantern, is a gallery with an iron balustrade, the view from this elevation upon the beach, the entrance of the Seine, Honfleur (where our Henry III is said to have fought the french armies, and to have distinguished himself by his valour) the distant hills of Lower Normandy, and the ocean, is truly grand. It brought to my mind that beautiful description of Shakspeare—

— — — — — — —The murmuring surge
That on th' unnumbered idle pebbles chafes,
Cannot be heard so high: I'll look no more,
Lest my brain turn, and the deficient sight
Topple down headlong.

We did not visit the other tower, as it was uniform with this. The woman who has the charge of the light, was very good humoured, and very talkative, she seemed delighted to show us every thing, and said she preferred seeing englishmen *in* her tower as friends, to the view she frequently had of them *from* it as enemies, alluding to the long, and masterly blockade of this port by a squadron of english frigates. She carried us to her little museum, as she called it, where she had arranged, very neatly, a considerable collection of fossils, shells, and petrefactions. Here she showed us with great animation, two british cannon balls, which during the blockade, had very nearly rendered her husband and herself, as cold and as silent as any of the petrefactions in her collection. In this little cabinet was her bed, where amidst the war of winds and waves, she told us she slept as sound as a *consul*.

In the basins of Havre, we saw several rafts, once so much talked of, constructed for the real, or ostensible purpose of conveying the invading legions of France, to the shores of Great Britain. I expected to have seen an immense floating platform, but the vessels which we saw, were made like brigs of an unusual breadth, with two low masts. The sincerity of this project has been much disputed, but that the french government expended considerable sums upon the scheme, I have no doubt.

I must not omit to mention, the admirable mode, which they have here, and in most parts of France, of constructing their carts. They are placed upon very high wheels, the load is generally arranged so as to create an equipoise, and is raised by an axle, fastened near the shafts. I was informed by a merchant, that a single horse can draw with ease thirty-six hundred weight, in one of these carts. These animals have a formidable appearance, owing to a strange custom which the french have, of covering the collar, with an entire sheep's skin, which gives them the appearance of having an enormous shaggy mane.

At night, we settled our bills which amounted to forty livres each. A considerable charge in this country, but we had lived well, and had not thought it worth our while, on account of the probable shortness of our stay, to bargain for our lodging, and board, a plan generally proper to be used by those, who mean to remain for some length of time, in any place in France.

Paris Diligence.

NOTES:

[2] The cruel imprisonment of la Fayette is alluded to.

CHAPTER IV.

Cheap travelling to Paris. — Diligences. — French Postilions. — Spanish Postilions. — Norman Horses. — Bolbec. — Natives of Caux. — Ivetot. — Return of Religion. — Santerre. — Jacobin. — The Mustard-pot. — National Property.

Before I proceed on my journey, I must beg leave to present a very cheap mode of travelling to Paris, from Havre, to those who have more time at their command than I had. It was given to me by a respectable gentleman, and an old traveller.

	Sols.
From Havre to Honfleur, by the passage-boat	10
From Honfleur to Pontaudemar, by land	3
From Pontaudemar to Labouille	3
From Labouille to Rouen, by water	12
From Rouen to Rolleboise, by land	6
From Rolleboise to Pontoise, by water	30
From Pontoise to Paris, by land	30

This progress, however, is tedious and uncertain.

At day-break we seated ourselves in the diligence. All the carriages of this description have the appearance of being the result of the earliest efforts in the art of coach building. A more uncouth clumsy machine can scarcely be imagined. In the front is a cabriolet fixed to the body of the coach, for the accommodation of three passengers, who are protected from the rain above, by the projecting roof of the coach, and in front by two heavy curtains of leather, well oiled, and smelling somewhat offensively, fastened to the roof. The inside, which is capacious, and lofty, and will hold six people with great comfort, is lined with leather padded, and surrounded with little pockets, in which the travellers deposit their bread, snuff, night caps, and pocket handkerchiefs, which generally enjoy each others company in the same delicate depositary. From the roof depends a large net work, which is generally crouded with hats, swords, and band boxes, the whole is convenient, and when all parties are seated and arranged, the accommodations are by no means unpleasant.

Upon the roof, on the outside, is the imperial, which is generally filled with six or seven persons more, and a heap of luggage, which latter also occupies the basket, and generally presents a pile, half as high again as the coach, which is secured by ropes and chains, tightened by a large iron windlass, which also constitutes another appendage of this moving mass. The body of the carriage rests upon large thongs of leather, fastened to heavy blocks of wood, instead of springs, and the whole is drawn by seven horses. The three first are fastened to the cross bar, the rest are in pairs, all in rope harness and tackling. The near horse of the three first, is mounted by the postilion, in his great jack boots, which are always placed, with much ceremony, like two tubs, on the right side of his Rosinante, just before he ascends. These curious protectors of his legs, are composed of wood, and iron hoops, softened within by stuffing, and give him all the dignity of riding in a pair of upright portmanteaus. With a long lash whip in his hand, a dirty night cap and an old cocked hat upon his head, hallooing alternately "à gauche, à droit," and a few occasional sacre dieus, which seem always properly applied, and perfectly understood, the merry postilion drives along his cattle. I must not fail to do justice to the scientific skill with which he manages on horseback, his long and heavy coach whip; with this commanding instrument, he can reanimate by a touch, each halting muscle of his lagging animals, can cut off an annoying fly, and with the loud cracking of its thong, he announces, upon his entrance into a town, the approach of his heavy, and clattering cavalcade. Each of these diligences is provided with a conducteur, who rides upon the imperial, and is responsible throughout the journey, for the comfort of the passengers and safety of the luggage. For his trouble the passenger pays him only thirty sols for himself, and fifteen more for the different postillions, to be divided amongst them, for these the donor is thanked with a low bow, and many "bien obligés," in the name of himself and his contented comrades.

Our companions proved to be some of our old friends the emigrants, who had thrown aside their marine dishabille, and displayed the appearance of gentlemen. We were much pleased with again meeting each other. Their conversation upon the road was very interesting, it was filled with sincere regret for the afflictions of their country, and with expressions of love and gratitude towards the english. They told us many little tales of politeness, and humanity which they had received from my countrymen in the various towns, where their destiny had placed them. One displayed, with amiable pride, a snuff box, which he had received as a parting token of esteem, another a pocket book, and each was the bearer of some little affectionate proof of merit, good conduct, or friendship.

One of these gentlemen, the abbè de l'H——, whose face was full of expression, tinctured with much grief, and attendant indisposition, with a manner, and in a tone, which were truly affecting, concluded a little narrative of some kindness which he had received, by saying, "if the english and my country are not friends, it shall not be for want of my prayers. I fled from France without tears, for the preservation of my life, but when I left England, I confess it, I could not help shedding some." They did not disgrace the generous abbè— such a nation was worthy of such feelings.

Our horses were of the norman breed, small, stout, short, and full of spirit, and to the honour of those who have the care of them, in excellent condition. I was surprised to see these little animals running away with our cumbrous machine, at the rate of six or seven miles an hour.

We traced the desolating hand of the revolution as soon as we ascended the first hill.

Our road lay through a charming country. Upon the sides of its acclivities, surrounded by the most romantic scenery of woods and corn fields, we saw ruined convents, and roofless village churches, through the shattered casements of which the wind had free admission.

We breakfasted at a neat town called Bolbec, seven leagues from Havre, where we had excellent coffee, butter, and rolls. All the household of our inn looked clean, happy, and sprightly.

This is the principal town of the province of Caux, the women of which dress their heads in a very peculiar, and in my humble opinion, unbecoming manner. I made a hasty sketch of one of them who entered the yard of the inn with apples for sale.

A Woman of the province of Caux in Normandy.

Such a promontory of cap and lace I never before beheld. She had been at a village marriage that morning, and was bedecked in all her finery. The people of this province are industrious and rich, and consequently respectable. At the theatre at Rouen I afterwards saw, in one of the front boxes, a lady from this country, dressed after its fashion; the effect was so singular that it immediately induced me to distinguish her, from the rest of the audience, but her appearance seemed to excite no curiosity with any other person. Our breakfast cost us each fifteen sous, to which may be added two sols more, for the maids, who waited upon us with cheerful smiles, and habited in the full cushvois costume, and which also entitled us to kisses and curtsies. I beg leave to oppose our breakfast charge to the rumours which prevailed in England, that this part of France was then in a state of famine. From this town, the road was beautifully lined with beech, chesnut, and apple trees. The rich yellow of the rape seed which overspread the surface of many of the fields on each side, was very animating to the eye. From this vegetable the country people express oil, and of the pulp of it make cakes, which the norman horses will fatten upon. We had an early dinner at Ivetot, five leagues distant from Bolbec. In ancient periods this miserable town was once the capital of a separate kingdom. In our dining room were three beds, or rather we dined in the bed room. I use the former expression out of compliment to the pride of our little host, who replied with some loftiness to one of our companions, who, upon entering the room, and seeing so many accommodations for repose, exclaimed, with the sharpness of appetite, "my good host, we want to eat, and not to sleep;" "gentlemen," said our mortified little maitre d'hôtel, "this chamber is the dining room, and it is thought a very good one." From its appearance I should have believed him, had he sworn that it was the state room of the palace of this ancient principality, of which this wretched town was once the capital. It reminded me of an anecdote related by an ancient english lady of fashion, when she first paid her respects to James I, soon after his accession to the crown of England. She mentions in her memoir, that his royal drawing room was so very dirty, that after the levee she was obliged to recur to her comb for relief. In plain truth, James I and his court were lousy.

Our master of the house was both cook and waiter. At dinner, amongst several other dishes, we had some stewed beef, I requested to be favoured with a little mustard, our host very solemnly replied, "I am very sorry, citizen, but I have none, if you had been fortunate enough to have been here about three weeks since, you might have had some." It was more than I wished, so I ate my beef very contentedly without it. With our desert we had a species of cake called brioche, composed of egg, flour, and water; it is in high estimation in France.

It was in this town *only* that I saw a specimen of that forlorn wretchedness and importunity, which have been said to constitute the general nuisance of this country.

In the shop of a brazier here, was exposed, a new leaden crucifix, about two feet and a half high, for sale; it had been cast preparatory to the reinauguration of the archbishop of Rouen, which was to take place upon the next Sunday week, in the great cathedral of that city.

In consequence of the restoration of religion, the beggars, who have in general considerable cleverness, and know how to turn new circumstances to advantage, had just learnt a fresh mode of soliciting money, by repeating the Lord's Prayer in French and Latin. We were treated with this sort of importunate piety for near a mile, after we left Ivetot.

I have before mentioned, that the barbarous jargon of the revolution is rapidly passing away. It is only here and there, that its slimy track remains. The time is not very distant when Frenchmen wished to be known by the name of Jacobins; it is now become an appellation of reproach, even amongst the surviving aborigines of the revolution. As an instance of it, a naval officer of rank and intelligence, who joined us at Ivetot, informed us, that he had occasion, upon some matters of business, to meet Santerre a few days before; that inhuman and vulgar revolutionist, who commanded the national guards when they surrounded the scaffold during the execution of their monarch. In the course of their conversation, Santerre, speaking of a third person, exclaimed, "I cannot bear that man; he is a

Jacobin." Let all true revolutionary republicans cry out, Bravo! at this.

This miscreant lives unnoticed, in a little village near Paris, upon a slender income, which he has made in trade, not in the *trade of blood*; for it appears that Robespierre was not a very liberal patron of his servants. He kept his blood-hounds lean, and keen, and poorly fed them with the rankest offal.

After a dusty journey, through a very rich and picturesque country, of near eighty miles, we entered the beautiful boulevards[3] of Rouen, about seven o'clock in the evening, which embowered us from the sun. Their shade was delicious. I think them finer than those of Paris. The noble elms, which compose them in four stately rows, are all nearly of the same height. Judge of my surprise—Upon our rapidly turning the corner of a street, as we entered the city, I suddenly found coach, horses and all, in the aisle of an ancient catholic church. The gates were closed upon us, and in a moment from the busy buzzing of the streets, we were translated into the silence of shattered tombs, and the gloom of cloisters: the only light which shone upon us, issued through fragments of stained glass, and the apertures which were formerly filled with it.

Rouen, from Mount St. Catherine.

My surprise, however, was soon quieted, by being informed, that this church, having devolved to the nation as its property, by force of a revolutionary decree, had been afterwards sold for stables, to one of the owners of the Rouen diligences.

An old unsaleable cabriolet occupied the place of the altar; and the horses were very quietly eating their oats in the sacristy!!

At the Bureau, we paid twelve livres and a half for our places and luggage from Havre to this town.

NOTES:

[3] Environs of a town, planted with stately trees.

CHAPTER V.

A female french fib. — Military and Civil Procession. — Madame G. — The Review. — Mons. l'Abbé. — Bridge of Boats. — The Quay. — Exchange. — Theatre. — Rouen. — Cathedral. — St. Ouens. — Prince of Waldec. — Maid of Orleans.

Having collected together all our luggage, and seen it safely lodged in a porter's wheelbarrow, Captain C. and I bade adieu to our fellow travellers, and to these solemn and unsuitable habitations of ostlers and horses, and proceeded through several narrow streets, lined with lofty houses, the shops of which were all open, and the shopkeepers, chiefly women, looked respectable and sprightly, with gay bouquets in their bosoms, to the Hôtel de l'Europe; it is a fine inn, to which we had been recommended at Havre, kept by Madame F——, who, with much politeness, and many captivating movements, dressed à-la-Grec, with immense golden earrings, approached us, and gave us a little piece of information, not very pleasant to travellers somewhat discoloured by the dust of a long and sultry day's journey, who wanted comfortable rooms, fresh linen, a little coffee, and a good night's repose: her information was, that her house was completely full, but that she would send to an upholsterer to fit up two beds for us, in a very neat room, which she had just papered and furnished, opposite to the porter's lodge (all the great inns and respectable townhouses in France have great gates, and a porter's lodge, at the entrance.) As we wished to have three rooms, we told her, we were friends of Messrs. G——, (the principal merchants of Rouen). She said, they were very amiable men, and were pleased to *send all their friends to her house* (a little french fib of Madame F——'s, by the by, as will appear hereafter); and she was truly sorry that she could not accommodate us better. We looked into the room, which also looked into the street, was exposed to all its noise, and very small. So we made our bows to Madame F——, and proceeded with our wheelbarrow to the Hôtel de Poitiers—a rival house. It is situated in the beautiful boulevards, which I have mentioned, and is part of a row of fine stonebuilt houses. Upon our ringing the bell, Madame P—— presented herself.

We told her, we were just arrived at Rouen, that we had the honour of being known to Messrs. G——, and should be happy to be placed under her roof, and wished to have two lodging rooms and a sitting room to ourselves. Madame P——, who possessed that sort of good and generous heart, which nature, for its better preservation, had lodged in a comfortable envelope of comely plumpness, observed, that Messrs. G—— were gentlemen of great respectability, were her patrons, and always *sent their* friends to *her* house (a point upon which these rival dames were at issue, but the truth was with Madame P——); that she would do all in her power to make us happy; but at present, on account of her house being very crowded, she could only offer us two bedrooms. We were too tired to think of any further peregrinations of discovery; so we entered our bed-rooms, which, like most of the chambers in France, had brick floors without any carpetting; they were, however, clean; and, after ordering a good fire in one of them (for the sudden and unusual frost, which, in the beginning of summer, committed so much ravage throughout Europe, commenced the day we had first the honour of seeing Madame P——); and, after enjoying those comforts which weary wanderers require, we mounted our lofty beds, and went to rest.

The next day we presented our letter, and ourselves, to Madame G——, the amiable mother of the gentlemen I have mentioned. She received us with great politeness, and immediately arranged a dinner party for us, for that day. It being rather early in the morning, we were admitted into her chamber, a common custom of receiving early visits in France.

About eleven o'clock we saw a splendid procession of all the military and civil authorities to the hôtel[4] of the prefect, which was opposite to our inn.

The object of this cavalcade was to congratulate the archbishop of Rouen (who was then upon a visit to the prefect, until his own palace was ready to receive him) on his elevation to the see.

This spectacle displayed the interference of God, in thus making the former enemies of his worship pay homage to his ministers, after a long reign of atheism and persecution.

About twelve o'clock, which is the hour of parade throughout the republic, we went to the Champ de Mars, and saw a review of the 20th regiment of chasseurs, under the command of generals St. Hiliare and Ruffin, who, as well as the regiment, had particularly distinguished themselves at Marengo.

The men were richly appointed, and in general well mounted. They all wore mustachios. They were just arrived from Amiens, where, as a mark of honour, they had been quartered during the negotiation.

The officers were superbly attired. St. Hiliare is a young man, and in person much resembles his patron and friend, the first consul; and, they say, in abilities also.

Some of the horses were of a dissimilar size and colour, which had a bad effect; but I was informed, upon making the remark, that they had lost many in battle, and had not had time properly to replace them. They were all strong and fiery, and went through their evolutions with surprising swiftness.

At dinner our party was very agreeable. Next to me sat a little abbè, who appeared to be in years, but full of vivacity, and seemed to be much esteemed by every person present. During the *time of terrour* (as the French emphatically call the gloomy reign of Robespierre) the blood of this good man, who, from his wealth, piety, and munificence, possessed considerable influence in Rouen, was sought after with keen pursuit. Madame G—— was the saviour of his life, by concealing him, previous to her own imprisonment, for two years, in different cellars, under her house, which she rendered as warm and as comfortable as circumstances, and the nature of the concealment, would allow. In one of these cells of humane secresy, this worthy man has often eaten his solitary and agitated meal, whilst the soldiers of the tyrant, who were quartered upon his protectress, were carousing in the kitchen immediately above him.

Soon after our coffee, which, in this country, immediately succeeds the dinner, we went to view the bridge of boats, so celebrated in history. This curious structure was contrived by an augustine friar named Michael Bougeois, it is composed of timber, regularly paved, in squares which contain the stones, and is 1000[5] feet in length; it commences from the middle of the quay of Rouen, and reaches over to the Fauxbourg of St. Sever, and carries on the communication with the country which lies south of the city. It was begun in the year 1626, below it are the ruins of the fine bridge of 13 arches, built by the empress Maud, daughter of Henry I of England. This ingenious fabric rests upon 19 immense barges, which rise and fall with the flowing and subsiding of the tide. When vessels have occasion to pass it, a portion of the platform sufficient to admit their passage is raised, and rolled over the other part. In the winter, when any danger is apprehended from the large flakes of ice, which float down the river, the whole is taken to pieces in an hour. The expense of keeping it in repair is estimated at 10000 livres, or 400 pounds sterling per annum, and is defrayed by government, it being the highroad to Picardy. Upon the whole, although this bridge is so much admired, I must confess it appeared to me a heavy performance, unsuitable to the wealth, and splendour of the city of Rouen, and below the taste and ingenuity of modern times. A handsome light stone structure, with a centre arch covered with a drawbridge, for the passage of vessels of considerable burden, or a lofty flying iron bridge, would be less expensive, more safe, and much more ornamental.

The view from this bridge up the Seine, upon the islands below mount St. Catharine, is quite enchanting. Upon the quay, although it was Sunday, a vast number of people were dancing, drinking, and attending shows and lotteries. Here were people of various nations, parading up and down in the habits and dresses of their respective countries, which produced quite the effect of a masquerade. The river Seine is so deep at this place, that ships of three hundred tons burden are moored close to the quay, and make a very fine appearance. The exchange for the merchants is parallel with the centre of the quay, and is a long paved building of about 400 feet in length, open at top, having a handsome iron balustrade, and seats towards the Seine, and a high stone wall towards the town. Over all the great gates of the city, is written, in large characters, "Liberty, Equality, Humanity, Fraternity or Death:" the last two words have been painted over, but are still faintly legible.

In the evening we went to the french opera, which was very crowded. The boxes were adorned with genteel people, and many beautiful young women. The theatre is very large, elegant, and handsome, and the players were good. I was struck with the ridiculous antics, and gestures of the chef in the orchestra, a man whose office it is to beat time to the musicians. In the municipality box which was in the centre, lined with green silk, and gold, were two fine young women who appeared to be ladies of fashion, and consequence; they were dressed after the antique, in an attire which, for lightness, and scantiness I never saw equalled, till I saw it surpassed at Paris. They appeared to be clothed only in jewels, and a little muslin, very gracefully disposed, the latter, to borrow a beautiful expression, had the appearance of "woven air."—From emotions of gratitude, for the captivating display which they made, I could not help offering a few fervent wishes, that the light of the next day might find them preserved from the dreaded consequences of a very bitter cold night.

Rouen, upon the whole, is a fine city, very large, and populous. It was formerly the capital of the kingdom of Normandy. It stands upon a plain, screened on three sides, by high, and picturesque mountains. It is near two leagues in compass, exclusive of the fauxbourgs of St. Severs, Cauchoise, Bouveul, St. Hiliare, Martainville and Beauvisme. Its commerce was very celebrated, and is returning with great rapidity. Most of the fine buildings in this city, and its environs are Anglo-Norman antiquities, and were founded by the English before they left Normandy.

The cathedral is a grand, and awful pile of gothic architecture, built by our William the Conqueror. It has two towers, one of which, is surmounted by a wooden spire covered with lead, and is of the prodigious height of 395 french feet, the other is 236 feet high.

The additional wooden spire, and the inequality of the towers produce rather an unfavourable effect. During the revolution, this august edifice was converted into a sulphur and gunpowder manufactory, by which impious prostitution, the pillars are defaced, and broken, and the whole is blackened, and dingy.

The costly cenotaphs of white marble, enriched with valuable ornaments containing the hearts of our Henry III, and Richard I, kings of England, and dukes of Normandy, which were formerly placed on each side of the grand altarpiece, were removed during the revolution.

The altarpiece is very fine. Grand preparations were making for the inauguration of the archbishop, which was to take place the following Sunday. There were not many people at mass; those who were present, appeared to be chiefly composed of old women, and young children. Over the charity box fastened to one of the pillars was a board upon which was written in large letters "Hospices reconnoissance et prospérité à l'homme généreux et sensible." I saw few people affected by this benedictory appeal. I next visited the church of St. Ouens, which is not so large as the cathedral, but surpasses that, and every other sacred edifice I ever beheld, in point of elegance. This graceful pile, has also had its share of sufferings, during the reign of revolutionary barbarism. Its chaste, and elegant pillars, have been violated by the smoke of sulphur and wood; and in many places, present to the distressed eye, chasms, produced by massy forges, which were erected against them, for casting ball. The costly railing of brass, gilt, which half surrounded the altar, has been torn up, and melted into cannon. The large circular stained window over the entrance called La Rose du Portail is very beautiful, and wholly unimpaired. The organs in all the churches are broken and useless. They experienced this fate, in consequence of their having been considered as fanatical instruments during the time of terrour. The fine organ of St. Ouens is in this predicament, and will require much cost to repair it[6].

I cannot help admiring the good sense which in all the churches of France is displayed, by placing the organ upon a gallery over the grand entrance, by which the spectator has an uninterrupted view, and commands the whole length of the interior building. In the English cathedrals, it is always placed midway between the choir and church, by which, this desired effect is lost. —St. Ouens is now open for worship.

In spite of all the devastations of atheistic Vandalism, this exquisite building, like the holy cause to which it is consecrated, having withstood the assailing storm, and elevating its meek, but magnificent head above its enemies, is mildly ready to receive them into her bosom, still disfigured with the traces of blind and barbarous ferocity.

Behind the altar, I met the celebrated prince of Waldec. He, who possessed of royal honours, and ample domains, revolted in the day of battle, from his imperial master, and joined the victorious and pursuing foe. I beheld him in a shaded corner of one of the cloisters of St. Ouens, in poor attire, with an old umbrella under his arm, scantily provided for, and scarcely noticed by his *new* friends. A melancholy, but just example of the rewards due to treachery and desertion.

I have described these churches only generally, it cannot be expected of me to enter into an elaborate history of them, or of any other public edifices. The detail, if attempted, might prove dull, and is altogether incompatible with the limited time, and nature of my excursion.

After we left St. Ouens, we visited the Square aux Vaux, where the celebrated heroine of Lorrain, Joan d'Arc, commonly called the Maid of Orleans was cruelly burnt at the stake, for a pretended sorceress, but in fact to gratify the barbarous revenge of the duke of Bedford, the then regent of France; because after signal successes, she conducted her sovereign, Charles, in safety, to Rheims, where he was crowned, and obtained decisive victories over the English arms. We here saw the statue erected by the French, to the memory of this remarkable woman, which as an object of sculpture seems to possess very little worthy of notice.

NOTES:

[4] Hôtel, in France, means either an inn, or private house of consequence.

[5] The french feet are to the english as 1068 to 1000.

[6] The ornaments of the churches of England experienced a similar fate from the commissioners of the Long Parliament, in 1643.

CHAPTER VI.

First Consul's Advertisement. — Something ridiculous. — Eggs. — Criminal Military Tribunal. — French Female Confidence. — Town House. — Convent of Jesuits. — Guillotine. — Governor W— —.

Upon looking up against the corner wall of a street, surrounded by particoloured advertisements of quack medicines, wonderful cures, new invented essences, judgments of cassation, rewards for robbers, and bills of the opera, I beheld Bonaparte's address to the people of France, to elect him first consul for life. I took it for granted that the spanish proverb of "tell me with whom you are, and I will tell you what you are," was not to be applied in this instance, on account of the company in which the *Consular application*, by a mere fortuitous coincidence, happened to be placed.

A circumstance occurred at this time, respecting this election, which was rather ridiculous, and excited considerable mirth at Paris. Upon the first appearance of the election book of the first consul, in one of the departments, some wag, instead of subscribing his name, immediately under the title of the page, "shall Napoleone Bonaparte be first consul for life?" wrote the following words, "I can't tell."

This trifling affair affords rather a favourable impression of the mildness of that government, which could inspire sufficient confidence to hazard such a stroke of pleasantry. It reached Mal Maison with great speed, but is said to have occasioned no other sensation there, than a little merriment. Carnot's bold negative was a little talked of, but as it was solitary, it was considered harmless. To the love of finery which the french still retain to a certain degree, I could alone attribute the gay appearance of the eggs in the market, upon which had been bestowed a very smart stain of lilac colour. The effect was so singular that I could not help noting it down.

On the third day after our arrival in this city, we attended the trial of a man who belonged to one of the banditti which infest the country round this city. The court was held in the hall of the ancient

41

parliament house, and was composed of three civil judges (one of whom presided) three military judges, and two citizens. The arrangements of the court, which was crowded, were excellent, and afforded uninterrupted accommodations to all its members, by separate doors and passages allotted to each, and also to the people, who were permitted to occupy the large area in front, which gradually rose from the last seats of the persons belonging to the court, and enabled every spectator to have a perfect view of the whole. Appropriate moral mottoes were inscribed in characters of gold, upon the walls. The judges wore long laced bands, and robes of black, lined with light blue silk, with scarfs of blue and silver fringe, and sat upon an elevated semicircular bench, raised upon a flight of steps, placed in a large alcove, lined with tapestry. The secretaries, and subordinate officers were seated below them. On the left the prisoner was placed, without irons, in the custody of two gendarmes, formerly called maréchaussées, who had their long swords drawn. These soldiers have a very military appearance, and are a fine, and valuable body of men. I fear the respectable impression which I would wish to convey of them will suffer, when I inform my reader, that they are servants of the police, and answer to our Bow-street runners. The swiftness with which they pursue, and apprehend offenders, is surprising. We were received with politeness, and conducted to a convenient place for hearing, and seeing all that passed. The accusateur general who sat on the left, wore a costume similar to that of the judges, without the scarf. He opened the trial by relating the circumstances, and declaiming upon the enormity of the offence, by which it appeared that the prisoner stood charged with robbery, accompanied with breach of hospitality; which, in that country, be the amount of the plunder ever so trifling, is at present capital. The address of the public accuser was very florid, and vehement, and attended by violent gestures, occasionally graceful. The pleaders of Normandy are considered as the most eloquent men in France, I have heard several of them, but they appear to me, to be too impassioned. Their motions in speaking frequently look like madness. He ransacked his language to furnish himself with reproachful epithets against the miserable wretch by the side of him, who with his hands in his bosom appeared to listen to him, with great sang froid. The witnesses who were kept separate, previous to their giving their evidence, were numerous, and proved many robberies against him, attended with aggravated breaches of hospitality. The court entered into proofs of offences committed by the prisoner at different times, and upon different persons. The women who gave their testimony, exhibited a striking distinction between the timidity of english females, confronting the many eyes of a crowded court of justice, and the calm self possession with which the french ladies here delivered their unperturbed testimony. The charges were clearly proved, and the prisoner was called upon for his defence. Undismayed, and with all the practised hardihood of an Old Bailey felon, he calmly declared, that he purchased the pile of booty produced in the court, for sums of money, the amount of which, he did not then know, of persons he could not name, and in places which he did not remember. He had no advocate. The subject was next resumed, and closed by the official orator who opened it. The court retired, and the criminal was reconducted to the prison behind the hall. After an absence of about twenty minutes, a bell rang to announce the return of the judges, the prisoner reentered, escorted by a file of national guards, to hear his fate. The court then resumed its sitting. The president addressed the unhappy man, very briefly, recapitulated his offences, and read the decree of the republic upon them, by which he doomed him to lose his head at four o'clock that afternoon.

It was then ten minutes past one!! The face of this wretched being presented a fine subject for the pencil. His countenance was dark, marked, and melancholy; over it was spread the sallow tint of long imprisonment. His beard was unshorn, and he displayed an indifference to his fate, which not a little surprised me. He immediately retired, and upon his return to his cell, a priest was sent for to prepare him for his doom. At present, in the provinces, all criminal offences are tried before military tribunals, qualified, as I have described this to be, by a mixture of civil judges and bourgeois.

It is one of the peculiar characteristics of such tribunals, to order immediate punishment after conviction. In the present instance, the fate of the offender was well known, for his crimes were many, and manifest, and as the interval allowed by military courts between the sentence, and its fulfilment, is so very short, the administrators of the law had postponed his trial for five months from the period of his commitment, for the purpose of affording him an indulgent procrastination. This mode, although arising from merciful motives, is, I am aware, open to objection; but it would be unfair to comment upon laws, which prevailed in times of revolution, and are permitted only to operate, until the fine fabric of french criminal jurisprudence, which is now constructing, shall be presented to the people. To the honour of our country, and one of the greatest ornaments of the british bar, the honourable T. Erskine, in the year 1789, furnished the french, with some of these great principles of criminal law, which it was impossible to perfect during the long æra of convulsion, and instability which followed, and which will constitute a considerable part of that great, and humane code, which is about to be bestowed upon the nation, and which will, no doubt, prove to be one of the greatest blessings, which human wisdom can confer upon human weakness.

Its foundation is nearly similar to that of our own. The great and enlightened genius whose name I have mentioned, has provided that the contumacy of *one* juryman shall not be able to force the opinion of the rest.

After the court had broken up, I visited the town house, which, before the revolution, was the monastery of the benedictines, who, from what appeared of the remains of their establishment, must have been magnificently lodged, and well deserved during their existence, to bear the name of the blessed. The two grand staircases are very fine, and there is a noble garden behind. Upon entering the vestibule of the council chamber, formerly the refectory, I thought I was going behind the scenes of a theatre. It was nearly filled with allegorical banners, pasteboard and canvas arches of triumph, altars, emblems of liberty, and despotism, and all the scenic decorations suitable to the frenzied orgies of a republican fête. Thank God! they appeared to be tolerably well covered with dust and cobwebs. At the end of this noble room, seated upon a high pedestal, was the goddess of liberty, beautifully executed in marble. "Look at that sanguinary prostitute," cried Mons. G——, to me, pointing to the statue, "for years have we

44

CHAPTER VII.

Filial Piety. — St. Catharine's Mount. — Madame Phillope. — General Ruffin's Trumpet. — Generosity. — Love Infectious. — Masons and Gardeners.

I have before had occasion to mention the humane conduct of Madame G—— towards the persecuted abbè; she soon afterwards, with the principal ladies of the city, fell under the displeasure of Robespierre, and his agents. Their only crime was wealth, honourably acquired. A committee, composed of the most worthless people of Rouen, was formed, who, in the name of, and for the use of the nation, seized upon the valuable stock of Messrs. G——, who were natives of France. In one night, by torchlight, their extensive warehouses were sacked, and all their stores were forcibly sold in the public marketplace to the best bidder: the plundered merchants were paid the amount of the sale in assignats, in a paper currency which then bore an enormous discount, and shortly afterwards retained only the value of the paper upon which the national note was written. In short, in a few hours an honourable family, nobly allied, were despoiled of property to the amount of 25,000*l.* sterling. Other merchants shared the same fate. This act of robbery was followed by an act of cruelty. Madame G——, the mother, who was born in England, and who married a French gentleman of large fortune, whom she survived, of a delicate frame and advanced in years, was committed to prison, where, with many other female sufferers, she was closely confined for eleven months, during which time she was compelled to endure all sorts of privations. After the committee of rapine had settled their black account, and had remitted the guilty balance to their employers, the latter, in a letter of "friendly collusion, and fraudulent familiarity," after passing a few revolutionary jokes upon what had occurred, observed that the G——s seemed to bleed very freely, and that as it was likely they must have credit with many persons to a large amount, directed their obedient and active banditti to order these devoted gentlemen to draw, and to deliver to them, their draughts upon all such persons who stood indebted to their extensive concern. In the words of a celebrated orator[7], "Though they had shaken the tree till nothing remained upon the leafless branches, yet a new flight was on the wing, to watch the first buddings of its prosperity, and to nip every hope of future foliage and fruit."

The G— —s expected this visit, and, by an ingenious, and justified expedient, prevented their perdition from becoming decisive.

Soon after the gates of the prison were closed upon Madame G— —, her eldest son, a man of commanding person, and eloquent address, in defiance of every friendly, and of every affectionate entreaty, flew to Paris.

It was in the evening of the last winter which beheld its snows crimsoned with revolutionary carnage, when he presented himself, undismayed, before that committee, whose horrible nature will be better described by merely relating the names of its members, then sitting, than by the most animated and elaborate delineations of all its deadly deeds of rapine and of blood. At a table, covered with green cloth, shabbily lighted, in one of the committee rooms of the national assembly, were seated Robespierre, Collot d'Herbois, Carnot, and David. They were occupied in filling up the lists for the *permanent* guillotine, erected very near them, in la Place de la Revolution, which the executioners were then clearing of its gore, and preparing for the next day's butchery. In this devoted capital more blood had, during that day, streamed upon the scaffold, than on any one day during the revolution.

The terrified inhabitants, in darkness, in remote recesses of their desolate houses, were silently offering up a prayer to the great God of Mercy to release them, in a way most suitable to his wisdom, from such scenes of deep dismay, and remorseless slaughter.

Robespierre, as usual, was dressed with great neatness and gayety; the *savage* was generally *scented*, whilst his associates were habited, en Jacobin, in the squalid, filthy fashion of that era of the revolution, in the dress of blackguards.

Mr. G—— bowed, and addressed them very respectfully. "I am come, citizens, before you," said this amiable son, "to implore the release of my mother; she is pining in the prison of Rouen, without having committed any offence; she is in years; and if her confinement continues, her children whose fortunes have been placed at the disposal of the national exigencies, will have to lament her death; grant the prayer of her son, restore, I conjure you, by all the rights of nature, restore her to her afflicted family." Robespierre looked obliquely at him, and with his accustomed sharpness, interrupted him from proceeding further, by exclaiming, "what right have *you* to appear before us, miscreant? you are an agent of Pitt and Cobourg (the then common phrase of reproach) you shall be sent to the guillotine—Why are you not at the frontiers?" Monsieur G——, unappalled, replied, "give me my mother, and I will be there to morrow, I am ready instantly to spill my blood, if it must be the price of *her* discharge." Robespierre, whose savage soul was occasionally moved by sights of heroic virtue, seemed impressed by this brave and unusual address. He paused, and after whispering a few words to his associates, wrote the discharge, and handing it over to a soldier, for the successful petitioner, he fiercely told him to retire.

Mr. G—— instantly set out for Rouen, where, after a long, and severe journey, he arrived, exhausted with fatigue, and agitation of mind; without refreshment, this excellent man flew to the gates of the prison, which contained his mother, and presented the discharge to the gaoler, who drily, with a brutal grin, informed him, that a trick had been played off upon him, that he had just received a counter order, which he held in his hand, and refused to release her!!!

It turned out, that immediately after Mr. G—— had left the committee room, the relenting disposition, which he had momentarily awakened in the barbarous breast of Robespierre, had subsided.

The generous sentiment was of a short, and sickly growth, and withered under the gloomy, fatal shade of his sanguinary nature. A chasseur had been dispatched with the counterorder, who passed the exulting, but deluded G—— on the road.

A short time after this, and a few days before Madame G——, and her unhappy companions were to have perished on the scaffold, the gates of their prison flew open, the world was released from a monster—Robespierre was no more.

This interesting recital I received from one of the amiable sufferers, in our way to St. Catharine's Mount. The story afforded a melancholy contrast to the rich and cheerful scenes about us.

From the attic story of a lofty house, built under this celebrated cliff, we ascended that part of it, which, upon the road to Paris, is only accessible in this manner. When we reached the top, the prospect was indeed superb; on one side we traced for miles, the romantic meanders of the Seine, every where forming little islands of poplars; before us, melting away in the horizon, were the blue mountains of Lower Normandy; at their feet, a variegated display of meadows, forests, corn fields, and vineyards; immediately below us, the city of Rouen, and its beautiful suburbs. This delicious, and expanded prospect, we enjoyed upon a seat erected near a little oratory, which is built upon the top of the mountain, resting, at one end, upon the pedestal of a cross, which, in the times of the revolution, had been shattered and overturned.

From this place, before dinner, we proceeded to la Montagne; a wild and hilly country, lying opposite to St. Catharine's. Here we were overtaken by a storm, upon which, a curé, who had observed us from his little cottage, not far distant, and who had been very lately reinstated in the cure of the church, in the neighbouring village, came out to us, with an umbrella, and invited us to dinner. Upon our return to our inn, to dress, we were annoyed by a nuisance which had before frequently assailed us. I knew a man, who in a moment of ill humour, vented rather a revengeful wish that the next neighbour of his enemy might have a child, who was fond of a *whistle* and a *drum*! A more insufferable nuisance was destined for us; the person who lodged in the next room to mine, was a beginner (and a dull one too) upon the *trumpet*. It was general Ruffin, whom I have mentioned before, forcing from this brazen tube, sounds which certainly would have set a kennel of hounds in a cry of agony, and were almost calculated to disturb the repose of the dead. General Ruffin, in all other respects, was a very polite, and indeed a very *quiet* young man, and a brave warrior; but in the display of his passion for music, I fear he mistook either his talent or his instrument. At one time we thought of inviting him to dine with us, that we might have a little respite, but after debating the matter well over, we conceived that to entertain an italian hero, as he ought to be received by those who admire valour even in an enemy, was purchasing silence at a very advanced price, so we submitted to the evil with that resignation which generally follows the incurable absence of a remedy. We now addressed ourselves to Madame P——, to know how long the general had learned the trumpet, and whether his leisure hours were generally occupied in this way. Madame P. was, strange to tell, not very able to afford us much information upon the subject. She was under the influence of love. The natural tranquillity of her disposition, was improved by the prospect of connubial happiness, which, although a widow, and touching the frontier of her eight and thirtieth year, she shortly expected to receive from the son of a neighbouring architect, who was then a minor. In this blissful frame of mind, our fair hostess scarcely knew when the trumpet of general R—— sounded. Her soul was in harmony with all the world, and it was not in the power of the demon of discord, nor even of this annoying brazen tube, to disturb her. Madame P—— well deserved to be blessed with such equanimity, and if *she* liked it, with such a lover, for she was a generous and good creature.

A gentleman to whom I was afterwards introduced, when the revolution began to grow hot, fled with his lady and his children into a foreign country, where, upon the relics of a shattered fortune he remained, until things wore a better aspect, and enabled him, with a prospect of safety, to return to his native country. In better times, upon his annual visits to a noble chateau, and large estates which he once possessed in this part of Normandy, he was accustomed to stop at the Hôtel de Poitiers. His equipage was then splendid, and suitable to his affluent circumstances. Upon his return to France, this gentleman, harassed by losses, and fatigued by sickness, arrived with his accomplished lady, and their elegant children, in a hired cabriole, at the gate of Madame P——. As soon as their name was announced, the grateful hostess presented herself before them, and kissing the children, burst into tears of joy; when she had recovered herself, she addressed her old patron, by expressing her hopes, that he had amended his fortune abroad, and was now returning to enjoy himself in tranquillity at home. "Alas! my good Madame P——," said this worthy gentleman, "we left our country, as you know, to save our lives, we have subsisted upon the remains of our fortune ever since, and have sustained heavy and cruel losses; we have been taken prisoners upon our passage, and are now returning to our home, if any is left to us, to solicit some reparation for our sufferings. Times are altered, Madame P——, you must not now consider me as formerly, when I expended the gifts of Providence in a manner which I hope was not altogether unworthy of the bounty which showered them upon me, we must bow down to such dispensations, you see I am candid with you; we are fatigued, and want refreshment, give us, my good landlady, a little plain dinner, such as is suitable to our present condition."

Madame P—— was so much affected, that she could make no reply, and left the room.

Immediately all the kitchen was in a bustle, every pot and pan were placed in instant requisition, the chamber-maids were sent to the neighbouring confectioners for cakes, and the porter was dispatched all over the city for the choicest fruits. In a short time a noble dinner was served up to this unfortunate family, followed by confectionary, fruits, and burgundy. When the repast was over, Mons. O—— ordered his bill, and his cabriole to be got ready. Madame P—— entered, and in the most amiable manner requested him, as she had exceeded his orders, to consider the dinner as a little acknowledgement of her sense of his past favours; money, though earnestly pressed upon her, she would not receive.

The whole of this interesting party were moved to tears, by this little act of nature and generosity. When they entered their carriage, they found in it bouquets of flowers, and boxes of cakes for the little children. No doubt Madame P—— moved lighter that day, than she ever did in her life, and perhaps found the remembrance of her conduct upon the occasion almost as exquisite as the hours of love, which she appeared most happily to enjoy, when we had the honour of being under her roof.

Monsieur O—— could not help exhibiting much feeling, when he related this little event to me. I must not fail to mention that all the house seemed, for the moment, infected with the happy disease of the mistress. General Ruffin's valet de chambre was in love with Dorothée, our chamber-maid; the porter was pining for a little black eyed grisette, who sold prints and pastry, in a stall opposite; and the ostler was eternally quarrelling with the chef de cuisine, who repelled him from the kitchen, which, in the person of the assistant cook, a plump rosy norman girl, contained all the treasure of his soul—love and negligence reigned throughout the household. We rang the bells, and sacre dieu'd, but all in vain, we suffered great inconvenience, *but who could be angry?* In the course of our walks, and conversations, with the workmen, whom we met, we found that most of the masons, and gardeners of Rouen, had fought in the memorable, bloody, and decisive battle of Marengo, at which it appears that a great part of the military of France, within four or five hundred miles of the capital, were present. The change they presented was worthy of observation; we saw men sun-browned in campaigns, and enured to all the ferocity of war, at the sound of peace assuming all the tranquil habits of ingenious industry, or rustic simplicity. Some of them were occupied in forming the shapeless stone into graceful embellishments for elegant houses, and others in disposing, with botanic taste, the fragrant parterre. After spending four very delightful days in this agreeable city, I bade adieu to my very worthy companion, captain W. C——, whose intention it was to spend some time here, and those friends, from whom I had received great attention and hospitalities, and wishing the amiable Madame P—— many happy years, and receiving from her the same assurances of civility, about seven o'clock in the evening I seated myself in the diligence for Paris, and in a comfortable corner of it, after we had passed the pavé, resigned myself to sleep.

NOTES:

[7] Vide Sheridan's oration against Hastings upon the Begum charge.

CHAPTER VIII.

Early dinner. — Mante. — Frost. — Duke de Sully. — Approach the Capital. —
Norman Barrier. — Paris. — Hôtel de Rouen. — Palais Royal.

At day break, the appearance of the country in all directions was delightful. The faint eastern blush of early morn, threw a mild, refreshing light over the moist and dew-dripping scenery.

The spirit of our immortal bard, awaking from the bosom of nature, seemed to exclaim—

————— Look love, what envious streaks
Do lace the severing clouds, in yonder east;
Night's candles are burnt out; and jocund Day
Stands tiptoe on the misty mountain tops.

About eight o'clock in the morning, we arrived at Mante, a picturesque town, built upon a fertile mountain, at the base of which the Seine flowed along, rippling against its many islands of beautiful poplars. At this hour, upon our alighting at the inn, we found a regular dinner ready, consisting of soups, meats, fowls, and confectionary. To the no small surprise of the host, I expressed a wish to have some breakfast, and at length, after much difficulty, procured some coffee and rolls.

The rest of the party, with great composure, tucked their napkins in the buttonholes of their waistcoats, and applied themselves to the good things before them, with very active address. What a happy race of people! ready for every thing, and at all times; they scarcely know the meaning of inconvenience.

In the midst of difficulty, they find accommodation; with them, every thing seems in harmony. After paying thirty sols for my repast, a charge which announced our approach to the capital, I walked on, and made my way to the bridge over another winding of the Seine, at the bottom of the town; which is a light, and elegant structure. The houses along the sides of the river are handsome, and delightfully situated. The principal church is a fine gothic building, but is rapidly hastening to decay; some of its pinnacles are destroyed, and all its windows broken in.

A small chapel, in the street opposite, which had an appearance of considerable elegance, was converted into a slaughter-house. Embosomed in woods, on the other side of the bridge, is a fine chateau, formerly belonging to the count d'Adhemar; here, while enjoying the enchanting prospect about me, I heard the jingling approach of our heavy diligence, in which, having reseated myself, we proceeded upon a fine high road, through thick rows of walnut, cherry, mulberry, and apple trees, for several miles, on each side of which, were vineyards, upon whose promising vintage, the frost had committed sad devastation. For a vast extent, they appeared blackened and burnt up. It was said that France sustained a loss of two millions sterling, by this unusual visitation.

In the course of our journey, I experienced in the conduct of one of our two female companions, an occurrence, allied to that, which is related by Sterne, of Madame de Rambouillet, by which he very justly illustrates the happy ease, with which the french ladies prevent themselves from ever suffering by inconvenient notions of delicacy.

A few miles from Mante, on the borders of the Seine, we passed one of the venerable chateaus of the celebrated duke de Sully, the faithful, able, and upright minister, of Henry IV of France, one of those great geniuses, who only at distant æras of time, are permitted to shine out amongst the race of men. Historians unite in observing that the duke performed all the duties of an active and upright minister, under a master, who exercised all the offices of a great and good king; after whose unhappy fate, this excellent man retired from the busy scenes of the world, and covered with time and honours expired in the eighty-second year of his age in the year 1641, at his castle of Villebon. The house is plain, and large. The grounds are disposed after the fashion of ancient times.

As we approached the capital, the country looked very rich and luxuriant. We passed through the forest of St. Germains, where there is a noble palace, built upon a lofty mountain. The forest abounds with game, and formerly afforded the delights of the chase to the royal Nimrods of France. Its numerous green alleys are between two and three miles long, and in the form of radii unite in a centre. The forest and park extend to the barrier, through which, we immediately entered the town of St. Germains, distant from Paris about twelve miles, which is a large and populous place, and in former periods, during the royal residence, was rich and flourishing, but having participated in the blessings of the revolution, presents an appearance of considerable poverty, and squalid decay. Here we changed horses for the last post, and ran down a fine, broad paved, royal road through rows of stately elms, upon an inclined plane, until the distant, and wide, but clear display of majestic domes, awful towers, and lofty spires, informed us that we approached the capital. I could not help comparing them with their cloud-capped brethren of London, over whose dim-discovered heads, a floating mass of unhealthy smoke, for ever suspends its heavy length of gloom. Our carriage stopped at the Norman Barrier, which is the grand entrance to Paris, and here presents a magnificent prospect to the eye. The barrier is formed of two very large, and noble military stone lodges, having porticoes, on all sides, supported by massy doric pillars. These buildings were given to the nation, by the national assembly in the year 1792, and are separated from each other, by a range of iron gates, adorned with republican emblems. Upon a gentle declivity; through quadruple rows of elms, at the distance of a mile and a half, the gigantic statues of la Place de la Concorde (ci-devant, de la Revolution) appear; beyond which, the gardens, and the palace of the Thuilleries, upon the centre tower of which, the tricoloured flag was waving, form the back scene of this splendid spectacle. Before we entered la Place de la Concorde, we passed on each side of us, the beautiful, and favourite walks of the parisians, called les Champs Elysées, and afterwards, on our left, the elegant palace of the Garde-meuble; where we entered the streets of Paris, and soon afterwards alighted at the bureau of the diligences; from which place, I took a fiacre (a hackney coach) and about six o'clock in the evening presented myself to the *mistress* of the hôtel de

Rouen, for the women of France generally transact all the masculine duties of the house. To this hotel I was recommended by Messrs. G——, upon mentioning whose name, I was very politely shown up to a suite of pleasant apartments, consisting of an antiroom, bedroom, and dressing-room, the two latter were charmingly situated, the windows of which, looked out upon an agreeable garden belonging to the palace of the Louvre. For these rooms I paid the moderate price of three livres a day. Here, after enjoying those comforts which travellers after long journies, require, and a good dinner into the bargain, about nine o'clock at night I sallied out to the Palais Royal, a superb palace built by the late duke d'Orleans, who when he was erecting it, publickly boasted, that he would make it one of the greatest brothels in Europe, in which prediction he succeeded, to the full consummation of his abominable wishes. This palace is now the property of the nation. The grand entrance is from the Rue St. Honorè, a long street, something resembling the Piccadilly of London, but destitute, like all the other streets of Paris, of that ample breadth, and paved footway, for the accommodation of pedestrian passengers, which give such a decided superiority to the streets of the capital of England. After passing through two noble courts, I entered the piazza, of this amazing pile; which is built of stone, upon arches, supported by corinthian pilasters. Its form is an oblong square, with gardens, and walks in the centre. The whole is considered to be, about one thousand four hundred feet long, and three hundred feet broad. The finest shops of Paris for jewellery, watches, clocks, mantuamakers, restaurateurs[8], china, magazines, &c., form the back of the piazza, which on all the sides, of this immense fabric, affords a very fine promenade. These shops once made a part of the speculation, of their mercenary, and abandoned master, to whom they each paid a rent after the rate of two or three hundred pounds sterling per annum. This place presents a scene of profligate voluptuousness, not to be equalled upon any spot in Europe. Women of character are almost afraid to appear here at noon day; and a stranger would conceive, that at night, he saw before him, one third of the beauty of Paris.

Under the roof of this palace are two theatres, museums of curiosities, the tribunate, gaming houses, billiard rooms, buillotte clubs, ball rooms, &c., all opening into the gardens, the windows of which threw, from their numerous lamps, and lustres, a stream of gay and gaudy light upon the walks below, and afforded the appearance of a vast illumination. At the bottom was a large pavilion, finely illuminated, in which were groups of people regaling themselves with lemonade, and ices. Upon this spot, in the early part of the revolution, the celebrated Camille Desmoulins used to declaim against the abuses of the old government, to all the idle and disaffected of Paris. It is said that the liveries of the duc d'Orleans gave birth to the republican colours, which used to be displayed in the hats of his auditors, who in point of respectability resembled the motley reformers of Chalk Farm. From the carousing rooms under ground, the ear was filled with the sounds of music, and the buzzing of crowds; in short, such a scene of midnight revelry and dissipation I never before beheld.

Upon my return to my hôtel, I was a little surprised to find the streets of this gay city so meanly lighted. Lamps placed at gloomy distances from each other, suspended by cords, from lofty poles, furnish the only means of directing the footsteps of the nocturnal wanderer.

NOTES:

[8] Restaurateur is now universally used instead of traiteur.

CHAPTER IX.

French Reception. — Voltaire. — Restaurateur. — Consular Guard. —
Music. — Venetian Horses. — Gates of the Palace. — Gardens of the
Thuilleries. — Statues. — The faithful Vase. — The Sabine Picture. —
Monsieur Perrègaux. — Marquis de Chatelet. — Madame Perrègaux. —
Beaux and Belles of Paris.

I forgot, in my last chapter, to mention that I paid for my place, and
luggage in the diligence, from Rouen to Paris, a distance of ninety
miles, twenty-three livres and eighteen sols. The next morning after
my arrival, and a good night's repose in a sopha bed, constructed
after the french fashion, which was very lofty, and handsome, and
very comfortable, I waited upon my accomplished friend, Madame
H——, in the Rue Florentine. I had the honour of knowing her when
in England, from very early years; I found her with her elegant and
accomplished daughter, in a suite of large rooms, very handsomely
furnished after the *antique*, which gives to the present fashionable
furniture of France, its form and character. These rooms composed a
floor of a noble stone built house, which contained several other
families; such is the customary mode of being lodged in the capital.
She received me in the most charming manner, and had expected me
for some days, previous to my arrival, and was that evening going to
her country house at Passi, a few miles from Paris, whither she
pressed me to accompany her, but I declined it, on account of the
short time which I had before me to spend in Paris. Madame H——
was not only a beauty, but a woman of wit and learning, and had
accordingly admitted Voltaire amongst the number of her household
gods; the arch old cynic, with his deathlike sarcastic face, admirably
represented, by a small whole length porcelain statue, occupied the
centre of her chimney piece. Upon finding that I was disposed to
remain in town, she recommended me to a restaurateur, in the
gardens of the Thuilleries, one of the first eating houses in Paris, for
society, and entertainment, to the master of which she sent her
servant, with my name, to inform him, that she had recommended
an english gentleman of her acquaintance to his house, and
requested that an english servant in his service might attend to me,

when I dined there. This was a little valuable civility, truly french. This house has been lately built under the auspices of the first consul, from a design, approved of by his own exquisite taste; he has permitted the entrance to open into the gardens of the consular palace. The whole is from a model of one of the little palaces of the Herculaneum, it is upon a small scale, built of a fine white stone, it contains a centre, with a portico, supported by doric pillars, and two long wings. The front is upon the terrace of the gardens, and commands an enchanting view of all its beautiful walks and statues. On the ground floor the house is divided into three long and spacious apartments, opening into each other through centre arches, and which are redoubled upon the view by immense pier glasses at each end. The first room is for dinner parties, the next for ices, and the third for coffee. In the middle is a flying staircase, lined on each side with orange trees, which ascends into a suite of upper dinner rooms, all of which are admirably painted after the taste of the Herculaneum, and are almost lined with costly pier glasses.

My fair countrywomen would perhaps be a little surprised to be told, that elegant women, of the first respectability, superbly dressed for the promenade, dine here with their friends in the public room, a custom which renders the scene delightful, and removes from it the accustomed impressions of grossness. Upon entering, the guest is presented with a dinner chart, handsomely printed, enumerating the different dishes provided for that day, with their respective prices affixed. All the people who frequent this place are considered highly respectable. The visitor is furnished with ice for his water decanters, with the best attendance at dinner, and with all the english and foreign newspapers. I always dined here when I was not engaged. After parting from Madame H——, who intended returning to town the next day, I went to see the consular guard relieved at the Thuilleries. About five companies of this distinguished regiment assemble in the gardens, exactly at five minutes before twelve o'clock, and, preceded by their fine band of music, march through the hall of the palace, and form the line in the grand court yard before it, where they are joined by a squadron of horse. Their uniform is blue, with broad white facings.

The consular guard were in a little disgrace, and were not permitted to do the entire duty of the palace at this time, nor during several succeeding days, as a mark of the first consul's displeasure, which had been excited by some unguarded expression of the common men, respecting his conduct, and which, to the jealous ear of a new created and untried authority, sounded like the tone of disaffection. Only the cavalry were allowed to mount guard, the infantry were, provisionally, superseded by a detachment from a fine regiment of hussars. On account of the shortness of this parade, which is always dismissed precisely at ten minutes past twelve o'clock, it is not much attended. The band is very fine, they had a turkish military instrument, which I never heard before, and was used instead of triangles. It was in the shape of four canopies, like the roofs of chinese temples, one above another, lessening as they ascended, made of thin plates of brass, and fringed with very little brass bells, it was supported by a sliding rod which dropped into a handle, out of which, when it was intended to be sounded, it was suddenly jerked by the musician, and produced a good effect with the other instruments. The tambour major is remarked for his noble appearance, and for the proportions of his person, which is very handsome: his full dress uniform on the grand parade is the most splendid thing, I ever beheld. The corps of pioneers who precede the regiment, have a singular appearance. These men are rather above six feet high, and proportionably made, they wear fierce mustachios, and long black beards, lofty bear skin caps, broad white leathern aprons, which almost touch their chins, and over their shoulders carry enormous hatchets. Their strange costume seemed to unite the dissimilar characters of high priest, and warrior. They looked like *military magi*. The common men made a very martial appearance. Their officers wore english riding boots, which had an unmilitary effect. Paris at present exhibits all the appearances of a city in a state of siege. The consular palace resembles a line of magnificent barracks, at the balconies, and upon the terraces of which, soldiers are every where to be seen lounging. This palace is partitioned between the first and second consuls, the third principal magistrate resides in a palace near the Louvre, opposite to the Thuilleries. The four colossal brazen horses, called the venetian horses, which have been brought from Venice, are mounted upon lofty pedestals, on each side of the gates of the grand court yard of the palace. When the roman emperor Constantine founded Constantinople, he attached these exquisite statues to the chariot of the Sun in the hippodromus, or circus, and when that capital was taken possession of by the venetian and french crusading armies, in 1206, the venetians obtained possession of them, amongst many other inestimable curiosities, and placed these horses in four niches over the great door of the church of St. Marco. Respecting their previous history, authors very much differ; some assert that they were cast by the great statuary Lysippus, in Alexander's time, others that they were raised over the triumphal arch of Augustus, others of Nero, and thence removed to the triumphal arch of Constantine, from which he carried them to his own capital.

They are said to be composed of bronze and gold, which much resembles the famous composition of the corinthian brass. Although these statues are of an enormous size, they are too diminutive for the vast pile of building which they adorn. The same remark applies to the entrance gates, of massy iron, which have just been raised by the directions of the first consul. The tricolour flag, mounted upon the centre dome of the palace, is also too small. From the court yard I entered the gardens, which are very beautiful, and about seven o'clock in the evening, form one of the favourite and fashionable walks of the parisians. They are disposed in regular promenades, in which are many fine casts from the ancient statues, which adorn the hall of antiques, and on each side are noble orange trees, which grow in vast moveable cases; many of these exotics are twenty feet high. Until lately many of the antiques were placed here, but Bonaparte, with his accustomed judgment and veneration for the arts, has had them removed into the grand national collection, and has supplied their places by these beautiful copies, amongst which I particularly distinguished those of Hippomanes, and Atalanta, for the beauty of their proportions, and the exquisite elucidation of their story. Here are also some fine basins of water, in the middle of which are jets d'eau. The gravel walks of the gardens are watered every morning in hot weather, and centinels are stationed at every avenue, to preserve order: no person is admitted who is the carrier of a parcel, however small. Here are groups of people to be seen, every morning, reading the prints of the day, in the refreshing coolness of the shade. For the use of a chair in the gardens, of which there are some hundreds, the proprietor is thankful for the smallest coin of the republic. At the bottom of the steps, leading to the terrace, in front of the palace, are some beautiful vases, of an immense size, which are raised about twelve feet from the ground: in one of them, which was pointed out to me, an unpopular and persecuted Parisian saved nearly all his property, during the revolution. A short time before the massacre of the 10th of August, 1792, when the domiciliary visits became frequent and keen, this man, during a dark night, stole, unobserved by the guards, into the garden, with a bag under his arm, containing almost all his treasure; he made his way to the vase, which, from the palace, is on the right hand, next to the Feuillans, and, after some difficulty, committed the whole to the capacious bosom of the faithful depositary: this done, he retreated in safety; and when the time of terrour was passed, fearful that he should not be able to raise his bag from the deep bottom of the urn without a discovery, which might have rendered the circumstance suspicious, and perhaps hazardous to him, he presented himself before the minister of the police, verified the narrative of the facts, and was placed in the quiet possession of his property, which in this manner had remained undisturbed during all that frightful period. From the gardens I went to the exhibition of David's celebrated painting of the suspension of the battle between the Sabines and the Romans, produced by the wives of the latter rushing, with their children in their arms, between the approaching warriors. David is deservedly considered as the first living artist in France, and this splendid picture is worthy of his pencil. It is upon an immense scale. All the Figures (of which there are many) are as large as life. The principal female raising her terrified infant, and the two chief combatants, are inimitable. I was informed, by good authority, that the court of Russia had offered 7000*l.* sterling for it, an unexampled price for any modern painting! but that David, who is very rich, felt a reluctance in parting with it, to the emperor, on account of the climate of Russia being unfavourable to colour.

From this beautiful painting, I went to pay my respects to Mons. O——, who resided at the further end of Paris, upon whom I had a letter of credit. Upon my arriving at his hotel, I was informed by the porter that his master was at his chateau, about ten miles in the country, with his family, where he lay extremely ill. This news rendered it necessary for me to leave Paris for a day and a night at least.

From Mons. O—— I went to Mr. Perregaux, the rich banker and legislator, to whom I had letters of introduction. He lives in the Rue Mont Blanc, a street, the place of residence of the principal bankers, and is next door neighbour to his rival Mons. R——, whose lady has occasioned some little conversation. Mons. P——'s hotel is very superb. His chief clerks occupy rooms elegantly fitted up, and decorated with fine paintings. He received me in a very handsome manner, in a beautiful little cabinet, adorned with some excellent, and costly paintings. After many polite expressions from him, I laughingly informed him of the dilemma in which I was placed by the unexpected absence of Mons. O——; upon which Mons. P—— in the most friendly manner told me that the letters which I had brought were from persons whom he highly esteemed; and that Mr. O—— was also his friend; that as it might prove inconvenient for me to wait upon him in the country, he begged to have the pleasure of furnishing me with whatever money I wanted, upon my own draughts. I felt this act of politeness and liberality very forcibly, which I of course declined, as I wished not only to take up what money I wanted in a regular manner, but I was desirous of seeing Mr. O——, who was represented to me as a very amiable man, and his family as elegant and accomplished. I was much charmed with the generous conduct of Mons. P——, from whom I afterwards received great attentions, and who is much beloved by the English. I felt it a pleasurable duty not to confine the knowledge of such an act of liberality to the spot where it was so handsomely manifested. The sessions of the legislative assembly had closed the day before my arrival, a circumstance I much regretted, as through his means I should have been enabled to have attended their sittings. The bankers of France are immensely rich, and almost command the treasury of the nation. Mons. P——, with the well-timed, silent submission of the flexible reed, in the fable, has survived the revolutionary storm, which by a good, but guiltless policy, has passed over him, without leaving one stain upon his honourable character, and has operated, like the slime of the Egyptian inundation, only to fructify, and increase his fortunes. He once however narrowly escaped. In the time of Robespierre, the Marquis de Chatelet, a few nights before his execution, attempted to corrupt his guards, and told them, if they would release him, Mons. P— — would give them a draft to any amount which they might choose then to name. The centinels rejected the bribe, and informed their sanguinary employer of the offer, who had the books of Mons. P— — investigated: he was in no shape concerned in the attempted escape; but hearing, with extraordinary swiftness, that the marquis, whose banker he had been, and to whom an inconsiderable balance was then due, had implicated him in this manner, he instantly with dexterity, removed the page which contained the last account of the unhappy nobleman, and also his own destiny, and thus saved his life. Mons. P— — is a widower; his daughter, an only child, is married to a wealthy general, a man of great bravery, and beloved by Bonaparte.

I dined this day at the Restaurateur's in the Thuilleries, and found the effect of Madame H— —'s charming civility to me. There were some beautiful women present, dressed after the antique, a fashion successfully introduced by David. This extraordinary genius was desirous of dressing the beaux of Paris after the same model; but they politely declined it, alleging that if Mons. David would at the same time create another climate, warmer, and more regular for them, they would then submit the matter to a committee of fashion. The women, though said, in point of corporal sufferance, to be able to endure less than men, were enchanted with the design of the artist, and, without approaching a single degree nearer to the sun, unmindful of colds, consumptions, and death, have assumed a dress, if such it can be called, the airiness of which to the eye of fancy, looked like the mist of incense, undulating over a display of beauty and symmetry, only to be rivalled by those exquisite models of grecian taste which first furnished them with these new ideas of personal decoration.

The French ladies every morning anoint their heads with the antique oil, scented; their sidelocks are formed into small circles, which just touch the bosom; and the hair behind is rolled into a rose, by which they produce a perfect copy of the ancient bust.

CHAPTER X.

Large Dogs. — A Plan for becoming quickly acquainted with Paris. — Pantheon. — Tombs of Voltaire and Rousseau. — Politeness of an Emigrant. — The Beauty of France. — Beauty evanescent. — Place de Carousel. — Infernal Machine. — Fouché. — Seine. — Washerwomen. — Fisherwomen. — Baths.

In the streets of Paris, I every where saw an unusual number of very large, fierce looking dogs, partaking of the breed of the newfoundland, and british bulldog. During the time of terrour, these brave and faithful animals were in much request, and are said to have given the alarm of danger, and saved, in several instances, the lives and property of their masters, by their accustomed fidelity. Upon my arrival in this great capital, I was of course desirous of becoming acquainted with its leading features as soon as possible, for the purpose of being enabled to explore my way to any part of it, without a guide. The scheme which I thought of, for this purpose, answered my wishes, and therefore I may presume to submit it to others.

On the second day after my arrival, I purchased a map of Paris, hired a fiacre, and drove to the Pantheon. Upon the top gallery which surmounts its lofty and magnificent dome, I made a survey of the city, which lay below me, like the chart with which I compared it. The clouds passed swiftly over my head, and from the shape of the dome, impressed me with an idea of moving in the air, upon the top, instead of the bottom of a balloon. I easily attained my object, by tracing the churches, the temple, the abbey, the palaces, large buildings, and the course and islands of the river, after which I seldom had occasion to retrace my steps, when I was roving about, unaccompanied. On account of no coal being used in Paris, the prospect was perfectly clear, and the air is consequently salubrious. The Pantheon, or church of St. Genevieve, is a magnificent building from the designs of Mons. Soufflet, one of the first architects of France: it was intended to be the rival of the St. Paul's of London; but, though a very noble edifice, it must fail of exciting any emotions of jealousy amongst the admirers of that national building. It is a magnificent pile, and when completed, is destined to be the principal place of worship, and is at present the mausoleum of the deceased great men of France. Upon the entablature over the portico is written, in immense characters, "AUX GRANDS HOMMES—LA PATRIE RECONNOISANTE." Parallel with the grand entrance, are colossal statues, representing the virtues imputed to a republic. Soon after the completion of the inner dome, about two years since, one of the main supporting pillars was crushed in several places by the pressure. The defective column has been removed, and until it can be replaced, its proportion of weight is sustained by a most ingenious and complicated wooden structure. Upon the spot where the altar is to be erected, I saw another goddess of liberty, with her usual appendages carved in wood, and painted, and raised by the order of Robespierre, for a grand revolutionary fête, which he intended to have given, in this church, upon the very day in which he perished. The interior dome is covered with two larger ones, each of which is supported by separate pillars, and pilasters, and the whole is constructed of stone only. The interior of the lower dome is covered with the most beautiful carvings in stone. The peristyle, or circular colonnade round the lower part of the exterior of the dome, is very fine, but I must confess, I do not like an ancient fashion which the french have just revived in their construction of these pillars, of making the thickest part of the column a little below the centre, and lessening in size to the base. Under this immense fabric are spacious vaults, well lighted; supported by doric pillars, the depositaries of the illustrious dead of France. At present there are only two personages whose relics are honoured with this gloomy distinction. Rousseau and Voltaire very quietly repose by the side of each other. Their remains are contained in two separate tombs, which are constructed of wood, and are embellished with various inscriptions. Hamlet's remark over the grave of Ophelia, strongly occurred to me.

"Where be your gibes now? your gambols? your songs? your flashes of merriment that were wont to set the table on a roar? not one now to mock your own grinning? quite chapfallen?"

At either end of the tomb of Jean Jacques, are two hands, darting out of the gates of death, supporting lighted torches, and below, (it is a little singular) are inscriptions illustrating the *peaceful*, and benevolent virtues of the enclosed defunct!

Peace to their manes! may they enjoy more repose, than that troubled world which their extraordinary, yet different talents seemed equally destined to embellish and to embroil, though it would be difficult to name any two modern writers, who have expressed, with more eloquence, a cordial love of peace, and a zealous desire to promote the interests of humanity!!

The church of St. Genevieve is entirely composed of stone and iron, of the latter very little is used. It has already cost the nation very near two millions sterling. As I was returning from the Pantheon, I was addressed by one of our emigrant companions, to whom I have before alluded. He had just arrived in Paris, intended staying about a month, and then returning to Toulon. He warmly made me an offer of his services, and during my stay here, sent every morning to know if he should attend me as a friendly guide, to conduct me to any place which I might wish to see, or to prevent me from suffering any imposition from tradesmen. His attentions to me were always agreeable, and sometimes serviceable, and strongly impressed upon my mind, the policy, as well as the pleasure, of treating every being with civility, even where first appearances are not favourable, and where an expectation of meeting the party again is not probable. In the course of the day I was introduced to Madame B— —, who resides, by permission of the first consul, in a suite of elegant apartments in the Louvre, which have been granted to her on account of her merits and genius, and also in consideration of the losses which she has sustained by the revolution. In her study she presented me to Mademoiselle T— —, the then celebrated beauty of Paris; her portrait by David, had afforded much conversation in the fashionable circles; she was then copying, with great taste, from the antique, which is generally the morning's occupation of the french ladies of fashion. She is certainly a very handsome young woman: but I think if the painter of France was to visit a certain western county of England, he would discover as many attractions for the display of his admirable pencil, as were at this time to be found in the study of Madame B— —. When we left her, Madame B— — asked me what I thought of her; I candidly made the above remark to her, "Ah!" said she, "you should have seen her about a month since, she was then the prettiest creature in all France;" how so, has she suffered from indisposition? "oh no," replied Madame B— —, smilingly, "but a *month*, you know, makes a considerable difference upon the face of beauty."

I was much obliged to Madame B— — for the remark, which is greatly within an observation which I have frequently made, on the evanescent nature of youthful beauty. Madame B— —'s calculations of the given progress of decay, were eighteen times more swift than mine. The subject of our conversation, and the busts by which we were surrounded, naturally led us to talk of the french ladies, and they reminded us, though *slightly*, of their present *dress*. Madame B— — entered into a particular account of the decorations of a lady of fashion in France. I have not patience enough to enumerate them here, except that the wife of a fournisseur will not hesitate paying from three to four hundred pounds for a Cachemire shawl, nor from four to five hundred pounds for a laced gown, nor a much larger sum for diamonds cut like pearls, and threaded. In this costly manner, does the ingenuity of art, and the prodigality of wealth do homage to the elegance of nature. The entrance to Madame B— —'s apartments seemed at first, a little singular and unsuitable, but I soon found that it was no unusual circumstance, after groping through dirty passages, and up filthy staircases to enter a noble hall and splendid rooms.

Upon leaving Madame B— — I passed the Place de Carousel, and saw the ruins of the houses, which suffered by the explosion of the infernal machine, which afforded so much conversation in the world at the time, by which the first consul was intended to have been destroyed in his way to the National Institute of Music. This affair has been somewhat involved in mystery. It is now well known that Monsieur Fouché, at the head of the police, was acquainted with this conspiracy from its first conception, and by his vigilant agents, was informed of the daily progress made in the construction of this destructive instrument, of the plan of which he had even a copy. The conspirators proceeded with perfect confidence, and as they thought with perfect security. Three days before it was quite completed, and ready for its fell purpose, from some surprise or dread of detection, they changed their place of meeting, and in one night removed the machine from the spot where it had been usually deposited. The penetrating eye of the police lost sight of them. Fouché, and his followers exercised their unrivalled talents for pursuit and discovery to no purpose. The baffled minister then waited upon Bonaparte, to whom he had regularly imparted the result of every day's information respecting it, and told him that he could no longer trace the traiterous instrument of his assassination, and requested him, as he knew it must be completed by this time, not to go to any public places, until he had regained a knowledge of it. Bonaparte replied, that fear only made cowards, and conspirators brave, and that he had unalterably determined to go with his accustomed equipage to the National Concert that very evening. At the usual hour the first consul set off undismayed from the Thuilleries, a description of the machine, which was made to resemble a water cask, being first given to the coachman, servants, and guards. As they proceeded, the advance guard passed it unobserved, but the coachman discovered it just as the consular carriage was on a parallel with it; instantly the dexterous and faithful charioteer lashed his horses into full speed, and turned the corner of the Rue Marcem. In one moment after, the terrible machine exploded, and covered the street with ruins. The thunder of its discharge shook the houses of Paris, and was heard at a considerable distance in the country. The first consul arrived in safety at the Hall of Music, and with every appearance of perfect tranquillity, entered his box amidst the acclamations of the crowded multitude. The range of buildings which was shattered by the explosion, has long offended the eye of taste, and presented a gloomy, and very inconvenient obstruction to the grand entrance of the palace. Bonaparte, with his usual judgment, which converts every event into some good, immediately after this affair, purchased the houses which were damaged, and the whole of this scene of ruins and rubbish is removing with all possible expedition, to the great improvement of this grand approach.

Whilst I was strolling along the banks of the Seine, I could not help remarking that it would suffer much by a comparison with the Thames, so finely described by sir John Denham—

Though deep, yet clear, though gentle yet not dull:
Strong without rage, without o'erflowing full.

The Seine is narrow, and very dirty; its waters, which are finely filtrated when drawn from the fountains of Paris, produce an aperient effect upon strangers, who are generally cautioned not to drink much of them at a time.

The tide does not reach further than several miles below Paris; to this cause I can alone attribute, though perhaps the reason is insufficient, that the river is never rendered gay by the passing, and repassing of beautiful pleasure boats, to the delights of which the parisians seem total strangers. Its shores are sadly disfigured by a number of black, gloomy, and unwieldy sheds, which are erected upon barges, for the accommodation of the washerwomen, who, by their mode of washing, which is, by rubbing the linen in the river water, and beating it with large flat pieces of wood, resembling battledores, until the dirt, and generally a portion of the linen retire together, make a noise very similar to that of shipwrights caulking a vessel. This is an abominable nuisance, and renders the view up the river, from the centre of the Pont de la Concorde, the most complete mélange of filth and finery, meanness and magnificence I ever beheld. Whilst I am speaking of these valuable, but noisy dames, I must mention that their services are chiefly confined to strangers, and the humbler class of parisians. The genteel families of France are annoyed by the unpleasant domestic occurrence of washing, when in town only once, and when in the country only twice in the course of the year. Their magazines of clothes are of course immense, for the reception and arrangement of which several rooms in their houses are always allotted. It is the intention of the first consul gradually to unkennel this clattering race of females, when it can be done with safety. To force them to the tub, and to put them into the suds too suddenly, might, from their influence amongst the lower classes of citizens, be followed by consequences not very congenial to the repose of the government.

To show of what importance the ladies of the lower class in Paris are, I shall relate a little anecdote of Bonaparte, in which he is considered to have exhibited as much bravery as he ever displayed in the field of battle.

The poissardes, whose name alone will awaken some emotion in the mind of the reader, from its horrible union with the barbarous massacres which discoloured the capital with blood during the revolution, have been from time immemorial accustomed, upon any great and fortunate event, to send a deputation of their sisterhood to the kings and ministers of France, and since the revolution to the various rulers of the republic, to offer their congratulations, accompanied by a large bouquet of flowers. Upon the elevation of Bonaparte to the supreme authority of France, according to custom, they sent a select number from their body to present him with their good wishes, and usual fragrant donation. The first consul sternly received them, and after rejecting their nosegay, fiercely told them to retire, and in future to attend to their husbands, their children, and their fisheries, and never more to attempt an interference in matters relating to the state. Upon which he ordered the pages in waiting to close the door upon them. He thought no doubt that "Omnium manibus res humanæ egent: paucorum capita sufficiunt." —"Human affairs require the hands of all, whilst the heads of few are sufficient."

These formidable dames, so celebrated for their ferocity, retired chagrined and chapfallen from the presence of the imperious consul, and have not attempted to force either their congratulations, or their bouquets upon any of the public functionaries since that period. Such a repulse as this, offered to a body of people, more formidable from their influence than the lazzaroni of Naples, would in all human probability have cost any one of the kings of France his crown. I received this anecdote from the brother of one of the ministers of France to whom this country is much indebted. Before the high daring of Bonaparte, every difficulty seems to droop, and die.

Near the Pont de la Concorde is a handsome, and ornamental building, which is erected upon barges, and contains near three hundred cold and tepid baths, for men and women. It is surrounded by a wooden terrace, which forms an agreeable walk upon the water, and is decorated with shrubs, orange trees, and flowers, on each side.

This place is very grateful in a climate which, in summer, is intensely warm. There are other public baths, but this is chiefly resorted to by people of respectability. The price is very moderate, thirty sols.

CHAPTER XI.

David. — Place de la Concorde. — L'Église de Madeleine. — Print-shops. —
Notre Dame. — Museum or Palace of Arts. — Hall of Statues. — Laocoon. —
Belvidere Apollo. — Socrates.

During my stay in Paris I visited the gallery of David. This celebrated artist has amassed a fortune of upwards of two hundred thousand pounds, and is permitted by his great patron, and friend Bonaparte, to occupy the corner wing of the old palace, from which every other man of genius and science, who was entitled to reside there, has been removed to other places, in order to make room for the reception of the grand National Library, which the first consul intends to have deposited there. His apartments are very magnificent, and furnished in that taste, which he has, by the influence of his fame, and his elegance of design, so widely, and successfully diffused. Whilst I was seated in his rooms, I could not help fancying myself a contemporary of the most tasteful times of Greece. Tunics and robes were carelessly but gracefully thrown over the antique chairs, which were surrounded by elegant statues, and ancient libraries, so disposed, as to perfect the classical illusion. I found David in his garden, putting in the back ground of a painting. He wore a dirty robe, and an old hat. His eyes are dark and penetrating, and beam with the lustre of genius. His collection of paintings and statues, and many of his own studies, afforded a perfect banquet. He was then occupied in drawing a fine portrait of Bonaparte. The presence of David covered the gratification with gloom. Before me, in the bosom of that art, which is said, with her divine associates, to soften the souls of men, I beheld the remorseless judge of his sovereign, the destroyer of his brethren in art, and the enthusiast and confidential friend of Robespierre. David's political life is too well known. During the late scenes of horror, he was asked by an acquaintance, how many heads had fallen upon the scaffold that day, to which he is said coolly to have replied, *"only one hundred and twenty!!* The heads of twenty thousand more must fall before the great work of philosophy can be accomplished."

It is related of him, that during the reign of the Mountain, he carried his portfolio to the front of the scaffold, to catch the last emotions of expiring nature, from the victims of his revolutionary rage.

He directed and presided at the splendid funeral solemnities of Lepelletier, who was assassinated by Paris, in which his taste and intimate knowledge of the ceremonies of the ancients, on similar occasions, were eminently displayed.

Farewell, David! when years have rolled away, and time has mellowed the works of thy sublime pencil, mayst thou be remembered only as *their* creator; may thy fame repose herself upon the tableau of the dying Socrates, and the miraculous passage of the Alpine hero, may the ensanguined records of thy political frenzy, moulder away, and may science, who knew not blood till thou wert known, whose pure, and hallowed inspirations have made men happier, and better, till thou wert born, implore for thee forgiveness, and whilst, with rapture she points to the immortal images of thy divine genius, may she cover with an impenetrable pall, the pale, and shuddering, and bleeding victims of thy sanguinary soul!

The great abilities of this man, have alone enabled him to survive the revolution, which, strange to relate, has, throughout its ravages, preserved a veneration for science, and, in general, protected her distinguished followers. Bonaparte, who possesses great taste "that instinct superior to study, surer than reasoning, and more rapid than reflection," entertains the greatest admiration for the genius of David, and always consults him in the arrangement of his paintings and statues. All the costumes of government have been designed by this artist.

David is not without his adherents. He has many pupils, the sons of respectable, and some of them, of noble families residing in different parts of Europe. They are said to be much attached to him, and have formed themselves into a military corps, for the purpose of occasionally doing honour to him, and were lately on the point of revenging an insult which had been offered to his person, in a manner, which, if perpetrated, would have required the interest of their master to have saved them from the scaffold.

But neither the gracious protection of consular favour, nor the splendour of unrivalled abilities, can restore their polluted possessor, to the affections and endearments of social intercourse. Humanity has drawn a *sable circle* round him. He leads the life of a proscribed exile, in the very centre of the gayest city in Europe. In the gloomy shade of unchosen seclusion, he passes his ungladdened hours, in the hope of covering his guilt with his glory, and of presenting to posterity, by the energies of his unequalled genius, some atonement for the havoc, and ruin of that political hurricane, of which he directed the fury, and befriended the desolations, against every contemporary object that nature had endeared, and virtue consecrated.

After leaving the gallery of David, I visited la Place de la Concorde. This ill fated spot, from its spaciousness, and beauty of situation, has always been the theatre of the great fêtes of the nation, as well as the scene of its greatest calamities. When the nuptials of the late king and queen were celebrated, the magnificent fireworks, shows, and illuminations which followed, were here displayed. During the exhibition, a numerous banditti, from Normandy, broke in upon the vast assemblage of spectators: owing to the confusion which followed, and the fall of some of the scaffolding, the supporters of which were sawed through by these wretches, the disorder became dreadful, and universal; many were crushed to death, and some hundreds of the people, whilst endeavouring to make their escape, were stabbed, and robbed. The king and queen, as a mark of their deep regret, ordered the dead to be entombed in the new burial ground of l'Église de Madeleine, then erecting at the entrance of the Boulevard des Italiens, in the neighbourhood of the palace, under the immediate inspection and patronage of the sovereign. This building was never finished, and still presents to the eye, a naked pile of lofty walls and columns. Alas! the gloomy auguries which followed this fatal spectacle, were too truly realized. On *that* spot perished the monarch and his queen, and the flower of the french nobility, and many of the virtuous and enlightened men of France, and in *this* cemetery, their unhonoured remains were thrown, amidst heaps of headless victims, into promiscuous graves of unslacked lime!

How inscrutable are the ways of destiny!

This spot, which, from its enchanting scenery, is calculated only to recall, or to inspire the most tender, and generous, and elegant sentiments, which has been the favoured resort of so many kings, and the scene of every gorgeous spectacle, was doomed to become the human shambles of the brave and good, and the Golgotha of the guillotine! In the centre, is an oblong square railing, which encloses the exact spot where formerly stood that instrument of death, which was voted permanent by its remorseless employers.

A temporary model in wood, of a lofty superb monument, two hundred feet high, intended to be erected in honour of Bonaparte and the battle of Marengo, was raised in this place, for his approval, but from policy or modesty, he declined this distinguished mark of public approbation. I was a little surprised to observe, in the windows of the principal print shops, prints exposed to sale, representing the late king, in his full robes of state, under which was written, Le Restaurateur de la liberté, (an equivoque, no doubt) and the parting interview between that unhappy sovereign and his queen and family in the temple, upon the morning of his execution.

This little circumstance will show the confidence which the present rulers feel in the strength and security of the present government; for such representations are certainly calculated to excite feelings, and to restore impressions which might prove a little hazardous to both, were they less powerfully supported.

I was also one morning a little surprised, by hearing from my window, the exhilarating song of "Rule Britannia" played upon a hand organ; upon looking down into the street, I beheld a Savoyard very composedly turning the handle of his musical machine, as he moved along, and a french officer humming the tune after him. Both were, no doubt, ignorant of the nationality of the song, though not of the truth of its sentiment.

In the course of one of my morning walks, I went to the metropolitan abbey of Notre Dame, which is situated at the end of a large island in the Seine, which forms a part of Paris, and is filled with long narrow streets. It is a fine gothic pile, but in my humble opinion, much inferior to our Westminster abbey, and to the great churches of Rouen.

From this building I visited, with a large party, the celebrated museum, or palace of the arts, which I afterwards generally frequented every other day.

This inestimable collection contains one thousand and thirty paintings, which are considered to be the chefs d'œuvre of the great ancient masters, and is a treasury of human art and genius, unknown to the most renowned of former ages, and far surpassing every other institution of the same nature, in the present times.

The first apartment is about the size of the exhibition room of Somerset house, and lighted as that is, from above. It contains several exquisite paintings, which have been presented to Bonaparte by the princes, and rulers of those states which have been either subdued by his arms, or have cultivated his alliance. The parisians call this apartment Bonaparte's nosegay. The most costly pictures in the room, are from the gallery of the grand duke of Tuscany. Amongst so many works, all exquisite and beautiful, it is almost temerity to attempt to select, but if I might be permitted to name those which pleased me most, I should particularize the Ecce Homo, by Cigoli Ludovico Cardi.

The breast of the mild and benevolent Saviour, striped with the bruises of recent punishment, and his heavenly countenance, benignly looking forgiveness upon his executioners, are beautifully delineated. L'Annonciation, by Gentileschi, in which the divine look of the angel, the graceful plumage of his wings, and the drapery of the virgin, are incomparable. La Sagesse chassant les Vices, which is a very ancient and curious painting, by Andrea Mantegna, in which the figure of Idleness, without arms, is wonderfully conceived. Les Noces de Cana, by Paul Veronese, which is considered to be the best of his works. It is the largest painting I ever beheld. The figures which are seated at the banquet, are chiefly the portraits of contemporary royal personages of different nations. From this room we passed into the gallery of the Louvre.

I cannot adequately describe the first impressions which were awakened, upon my first entering it, and contemplating such a galaxy of art and genius. This room is one thousand two hundred feet long, and is lined with the finest paintings of the french, flemish, and italian schools, and is divided by a curious double painting upon slate, placed upon a pedestal in the middle of the room, which represents the front and back view of the same figures.

The first division of this hall contains the finest works of le Brun, many of which are upon an immense scale. L'Hyver ou le Deluge, by Poussin, is truly sublime, but is unfortunately placed in a bad light. There are also some beautiful marine paintings, by Verney. Les Religieuses, by Philipe de Champagne, is justly celebrated for the principal figure of the dying nun. Vue de Chevet d'une eglise, by Emanuel de Witte, is an exquisite little cabinet picture, in which the effect of a ray of light shining through a painted window, upon a column, is inimitable, and the perspective is very fine. There are here also some of the finest works of Wouvermans, and a charming picture by Teniers. La Vierge, l'enfant Jesus, la Madeleine, et St. Jerome, by Antoine Allegri Correge, is considered to be a picture of great beauty and value. There are also some glorious paintings by Reubens. I have thus briefly selected these pictures from the rest, hoping, at the same time, that it will not be inferred that those which I have not named, of which it would be impossible to offer a description without filling a bulky volume, are inferior to the works which I have presumed to mention. The recording pen must rival that matchless pencil, which has thus adorned the walls of the Museum, before it can do justice to such a magnificent collection.

This exhibition is public three days in the week, and at other times is open to students and to strangers, upon their producing their passports. On public days, all descriptions of persons are here to be seen. The contemplation of such a mixture is not altogether uninteresting.

The sun-browned rugged plebeian, whose mind, by the influence of an unexampled political change, has been long alienated from all the noble feelings which religion and humanity inspire, is here seen, with his arms rudely folded over his breast, softening into pity, before the struggling and sinking sufferers of a deluged world, or silently imbibing from the divine resigned countenance of the crucified Saviour, a hope of unperishable bliss, beyond the grave. Who will condemn a policy by which ignorance becomes enlightened, profligacy penitent, and which, as by stealth, imparts to the relenting bosom of ferocity the subdued, and social dispositions of *true* fraternity?

To amuse, may be necessary to the present government of France, but surely to supplant the wild abandoned principles of a barbarous revolution, with *new* impressions, created by an unreserved display of the finest and most persuasive images of resigned suffering, heroic virtue, or elegant beauty, cannot be deemed unworthy of the ruler of a great people.

At this place, as well as at all the other national exhibitions, no money for admission is required or expected. No person is admitted with a stick, and guards attend to preserve the pictures from injury, and the exhibition from riot. The gallery of the Louvre is at present, unfortunately, badly lighted throughout, owing to the light issuing chiefly on one side, from long windows. This inconvenience, however, is soon to be remedied; by observing the same manner of lighting, as in the adjoining apartment.

From the museum, we descended into la Salle des Antiques, which contains all the treasury of grecian and roman statuary. The first object to which we hastened, was the statue of Laocoon, for so many ages, and by so many writers admired and celebrated. This superb specimen of grecian sculpture, is supposed to be the united production of Polydorus, Athenodorus, and Agesander, but its great antiquity renders its history somewhat dubious. In the beginning of the sixteenth century it was discovered at Rome amongst the ruins of the palace of Titus, and deposited in the Farnese palace, whence it has been removed to Paris, by the orders of Bonaparte, after the conquest of Italy. It represents Laocoon, the priest of Apollo and Neptune, and his two sons writhing in the folds of two hideous serpents. The reader will remember the beautiful lines of Virgil upon the subject,

"— — — — — — — —et primum parva duorum
Corpora natorum serpens amplexus uterque
Implicat, et miseros morsu depascitur artus.
Post, ipsum auxilio subeuntem ac tela ferentem
Corripiunt, spirisque ligant ingentibus: et jam
Bis medium amplexi, bis collo squamea circum
Terga dati, superant capite et cervicibus altis.
Ille simul manibus tendit divellere nodos—"

Or, in the english habit which Dryden has given them,

"And first around the tender boys they wind,
Then with their sharpen'd fangs, their limbs and bodies grind.
The wretched father, running to their aid,
With pious haste, but vain, they next invade:
Twice round his waist the winding volumes roll'd,
And twice about his gasping throat they fold.
The priest, thus doubly chok'd, their crests divide,
And tow'ring o'er his head in triumphs ride.
With both his hands he labours at the knots—"

Pliny mentions this statue as the admiration of the age in which he flourished.

I fear that I shall be guilty of a sort of profanation when I remark, that the figures of the two sons of Laocoon appear to exhibit rather more marks of maturity, and strength of muscle than are natural to their size, and to the supposed tenderness of their age. It is, however, a glorious work of art.

We next beheld the Belvidere Apollo. This statue, in my humble opinion, surpasses every other in the collection. All the divinity of a god beams through this unrivalled perfection of form. It is impossible to impart the impressions which it inspires. The rivetted beholder is ready to exclaim, with Adam, when he first discerns the approach of Raphael,

> "————————behold what glorious shape
> Comes this way moving: seems another morn,
> Risen on mid-noon; some great behest from Heav'n."

The imagination cannot form such an union of grace and strength. During my stay in Paris, I frequently visited this distinguished statue, and discovered fresh subjects of amazement, and admiration as often as I gazed upon it. One of its remarkable beauties, is its exquisite expression of motion. Its aerial appearance perpetually excites the idea of its being unstationary, and unsupported. As it would be a rash, and vain attempt to give a complete description of this matchless image, I must, reluctantly, leave it, to inform my reader, that on the other side of the Hall are the original Diana (which is wonderfully fine) and several very beautiful Venuses. The Venus de Medicis is not here. There are also some fine whole length statues of roman magistrates, in their curule chairs.

In the Temple of the Muses, are exquisite busts of Homer and Socrates. Pliny informs us that the ancient world possessed no original bust of the former. That of the latter seems to have been chisseled to represent the celebrated athenian before he had obtained his philosophical triumph over those vices, which a distinguished physiognomist of his time once imputed to him from the character of his features.

CHAPTER XII.

Bonaparte. — Artillery. — Mr. Pitt — Newspapers. — Archbishop of Paris. —
Consular Colours. — Religion. — Consular Conversion. — Madame
Bonaparte. — Consular Modesty. — Separate Beds. — A Country Scene. —
Connubial Affection. — Female Bravery.

A little anecdote is related of Bonaparte, which unfolded the bold, and daring character of this extraordinary man in early life: when he was about fifteen years of age, and a cadet in the military school at Paris—by the by, the small distance between this seminary and his present palace, and the swiftness of his elevation, afford a curious coincidence—in the vast plain of the Champ de Mars, the court, and the parisians were assembled to witness the ascent of a balloon. Bonaparte made his way through the crowd, and unperceived, entered the inner fence, which contained the apparatus for inflating the silken globe. It was then very nearly filled, and restrained from its flight by the last cord only. The young cadet requested the aeronaut to permit him to mount the car with him; which request was immediately refused, from an apprehension that the feelings of the boy might embarrass the experiment. Bonaparte is reported to have exclaimed, "I am young, it is true, but I neither fear the powers of earth, nor of air," and sternly added, "will you let me ascend?" The aeronaut, a little offended at his obtrusion, sharply replied, "No, Sir, I will not; I beg that you will retire." Upon which the little enraged officer, drew a small sabre, which he wore with his uniform, instantly cut the balloon in several places, and destroyed the curious apparatus, which the aeronaut had constructed, with infinite labour and ingenuity, for the purpose of trying the possibility of aerial navigation.

Paris was almost unpeopled this day, to view the spectacle. The disappointment of the populace, which was said to have exceeded seven hundred thousand persons, became violent and universal. The king sent to know the reason of the tumult, when the story was related to him, the good humoured monarch laughed heartily, and said, "Upon my word that impetuous boy, will make a brave officer."—The devoted king little thought that he was speaking of his successor.—The young offender was put under arrest, and confined for four days.

This man is certainly the phenomenon of the present times. It is a circumstance worthy of remark, that the artillery has furnished France with most of its present distinguished heroes, who have also been bred up in the same military school with Bonaparte. A short time before my arrival at Paris, this great genius, who displays a perfect knowledge of mankind, and particularly of the people over whom he rules, discovered that the parisians, from a familiarity with his person, and from his lady and his family having occasionally joined in their parties of amusement, began to lose that degree of awe and respect for him, which he so well knows how to appreciate, as well as to inspire. In consequence of this, he gradually retired from every circle of fashion, and was at this period, almost as inaccessible as a chinese emperor. The same line of conduct was also adopted by the principal officers of government. He resided almost wholly at Mal Maison, except on state days, when only those strangers were permitted to be introduced to him, who had satisfired the ambassadors of their respective nations, that they had been previously presented at their own courts. If Bonaparte is spared from the stroke of the assassin, or the prætorian caprice of the army, for any length of time, he will have it in his power to augment the services which he has already afforded to the republic, by rebuilding the political edifice of France, with many meliorations, for which some materials may be collected from her own ruins, and some from the tried and approved constitutions of other countries. If his ambition will permit him to discharge this great undertaking faithfully, in a manner uniform with that glory which he has acquired in the field, and influenced only by the noble desire of giving rational liberty, and practicable happiness to the people over whom he sways, they will in return, without jealousy or regret, behold the being to whose wisdom and moderation they will be thus indebted, led to the highest seat amongst them—they will confer those sanctions upon his well merited distinction, without which all authority is but disastrous usurpation—a comet's blaze, flaming in a *night of dismay*, and *setting in gloom*.

The dignity of such a legislator will be self-maintained, and lasting. Upon him, the grateful french will confer those unforced, unpurchased suffrages, which will *prevent* that fate, which, in their absence, the subtilty of policy, the fascinations of address, the charm of corruption, and even the terror of the bayonet can only *postpone.—* Yes, Bonaparte! millions of suffering beings, raising themselves from the dust, in which a barbarous revolution has prostrated them, look up to thee for liberty, protection, and repose. They *will* not look to thee in vain. The retiring storm still flashing its lessening flame, and rolling its distant thunders will teach thee, *were it necessary*, not to force them to remeasure their vengeance by their wrongs.

In Paris, the achievements of the first consul are not much talked of, so true is the old adage, that no man is a hero to his own domestic. The beauties of a colossal statue, must be contemplated at a distance.

The french at present work, walk, eat, drink, and sleep in tranquillity, and what is of more consequence to them, they dance in security, to which may be added, that their taxes are neither very heavy, nor oppressive. In every party which I entered, I found the late minister of Great Britain was the prevailing subject of curiosity. I was overpowered with questions respecting this great man, which in their minute detail, extended to ascertain what was the colour of his eye, the shape of his nose, and whether in a morning he wore hussar boots, or shoes. This little circumstance could not fail of proving pleasant to an englishman. They informed me, that throughout the war, they regularly read in their own diurnal prints, our parliamentary debates, and the general outline of most of our political schemes, which were furnished by people in the pay of the french government, who resided in England notwithstanding the severity of the legislative, and the vigilance of the executive authorities. Whilst I am mentioning the subject of newspaper intercourse, I cannot help lamenting, that since the renewal of national friendship, the public prints of both countries are not more under the influence of cordiality and good humour.

The liberty of the press is the palladium of reason, the distributor of light and learning, the public and undismayed assertor of interdicted truth. It is the body and the *honour guard* of civil and political liberty. Where the laws halt with dread, the freedom of the press advances, and with the subtle activity of conscience, penetrates the fortified recesses and writes its *fearful sentence on the palace wall* of recoiling tyrants. As an englishman, my expiring sigh should be breathed for its preservation; but as an admirer of social repose and national liberality, I regret to see its noble energies engaged in the degrading service of fretful spleen, and ungenerous animadversion. When the horizon is no longer blackened with the smoke of the battle, it is unworthy of two mighty empires to carry on an ignoble war of words. If peace is their wish, let them manifest the great and enlightened sentiment in all its purity, and disdain to irritate each other by acts of petulant and provoking recrimination.

A short time preceding my arrival in France, Bonaparte had rendered himself very popular amongst the constitutional clergy, by a well timed compliment to the metropolitan archbishop. The first consul gave a grand dinner to this dignified prelate, and to several of his brethren. After the entertainment, Bonaparte addressed the archbishop by observing, that as he had given directions for the repairing of the archiepiscopal palace, he should very much like to take a ride in the archbishop's carriage, to see the progress which the workmen had made. The prelate bowed to the first consul, and informed him that he had no carriage, otherwise he should be much flattered by conducting him thither. Bonaparte good humouredly said, "how can that be? your coach has been waiting at the gate this half hour," and immediately led the venerable archbishop down the steps of the Thuilleries, where he found a plain handsome carriage, with a valuable pair of horses, and a coachman, and footmen dressed in the livery which Bonaparte had just before informed him would be allotted to him, when his establishment was completed. The whole was a present from the private purse of the first consul. Upon their arrival at the palace, the archbishop was agreeably surprised by finding that the most minute, and liberal attention had been paid to his comfort and accommodation.

The clergy seem to be in favour with Bonaparte. When he assisted in the last spring at the inauguration of the archbishop of Paris, in the metropolitan church of Notre Dame, and gave to the restoration of religion "all the circumstance of pomp" and military parade, he was desirous of having the colours of his regiment consecrated by the holy prelate, and submitted his wishes to his soldiers. A few days afterwards, a deputation waited upon their general in chief, with this reply, "Our banners have already been consecrated by the blood of our enemies at Marengo; the benediction of a priest cannot render them more sacred in our eyes, nor more animating in the time of battle." Bonaparte prudently submitted himself to their prætorian resolution, and the consular colours remain to this hour in the same *unchristianlike* condition, as when they first waved at the head of their victorious legions. This anecdote will in some degree prove a fact which, notwithstanding the counter reports of english newspapers, I found every where confirmed, that although religion is *new* to the french, yet that the novelty has at present but little charm for them. I had frequent opportunity of making this remark, as well in the capital as in the departments of the republic through which I passed. In Paris, the Sabbath can only be considered as a day of dissipation to the lovers of gayety, and a day of unusual profit to the man of trade. Here, it is true, upon particular festival days, considerable bodies of people are to be seen in the act of worship, but curiosity, and the love of show assemble them together, if it was otherwise their attendance would be more numerous and regular. The first consul does not seem to possess much fashionable influence over the french in matters of religion, otherwise, as he has the credit of attending mass, with very pious punctuality, in his private chapel at Mal Maison, it might be rather expected, that devotion would become a little more familiar to the people.

Upon another subject, the *will* of the chief magistrate has been equally unfortunate. To the few ladies who are admitted into his social circles, he has declared himself an enemy to that dress, or undress (I am puzzled to know what to call it) which his friend, David, has, so successfully, recommended, for the purpose of displaying, with the least possible restraint, the fine proportions of the female form. Madame Bonaparte, who is considered to be in as good a state of subordination to her *young* husband, as the consular regiment is to their *young* general, contrives to exhibit her elegant person to great advantage; by adopting a judicious and graceful medium of dress, by which she tastefully avoids a load of decoration, which repels the eye by too dense a covering, and that questionable airiness of ornament which, by its gracious and unrestrained display, deprives the imagination of more than half its pleasures. Bonaparte is said not to be indifferent to those affections which do honour to the breast which cherishes them, nor to the morals of the people whom he governs.

It is well known that in France, in the house of a new fashionable couple, *separate chambers* are always reserved for the *faithful* pair, which after the solemnities of marriage very seldom remain long unoccupied. The first consul considers such separations as unfriendly to morals. A few months since, by a well timed display of assumed ignorance, he endeavoured to give fashion to a sentiment which may in time reduce the number of these *family accommodations*. The noble palace of St. Cloud was at this time preparing for him; the principal architect requested of him to point out in what part of the palace he would wish to have his separate sleeping room. "I do not know what you mean," said the young imperial philosopher, "crimes only divide the husband from his wife. Make as many bed rooms as you please, but only *one* for me and Madame Bonaparte."

I must now quit the dazzling splendour of imperial virtues for the more tranquil, but not less fascinating appearance of retired and modest merit.

It was in the afternoon of one of the finest days in June, when Madame O— —, with her nephew, a very amiable young man, called in their carriage and took me to the chateau of her husband, to whom I had letters of introduction. After passing through a charming country for nine miles, adorned on each side with gardens and country houses, we arrived at the pleasant village of la Reine. As soon as we entered it, the sight of the carriage, and of their benefactress, seemed to enliven the faces of the villagers, who were seated in picturesque groupes at the doors of their cottages. Such animated looks were not lighted up by curiosity, for they had seen Madame O— — a thousand and a thousand times, but because they had seldom seen her without experiencing some endearing proof of her bountiful heart. We left the village to the right, and proceeded through a private road, lined with stately walnut trees, of nearly a mile in length, which led to Monsieur O——'s. It was evening; the sky was cloudless, the sun was setting in great glory, and covered the face of this romantic country with the richest glow. Near the gate of a shrubbery I beheld a very handsome boy, whose appearance at once bespoke him to be the son of a gentleman, the animated smile of Madame O——, immediately convinced me that it was her son; "see," said the delighted mother, "it is my little gardener;" the little graceful rustic had a small spade in his hand, which he threw down, and ran to us. We alighted at the entrance of the garden, into which we entered, under a beautiful covered treillage, lined with jessamine and honeysuckles. At the end were two elegant young women, waiting, with delight, to receive their mother, from whom they had been separated only a few hours. With this charming family I entered the house, which was handsome but plain. The hospitable owner rose from his sofa, and, after embracing his elegant lady with great affection, he received me with all the expressions and warmth of a long friendship. Soon afterwards his servant (a faithful indian) entered, and spread upon the table, Madeira, Burgundy, and dried fruits. It was intensely hot: the great window at the end of the room in which we were sitting, opened into the gardens, which appeared to be very beautiful, and abounded with nightingales, which were then most sweetly singing. "They are my little musicians," said Monsieur O——, "we have made a pleasant bargain together, I give them crumbs of bread and my bowers to range in, and they give me this charming music every evening."

Monsieur O—— was an invalide, the revolution, poignant vexations, heavy losses, and a painful separation from his native country, for the preservation of his life, and that of his family, had undermined his health. Grief had made sad inroads upon a delicate constitution. It was his good fortune to be the husband of one of the finest, and most amiable women in France, and the father of an affectionate, beautiful, and accomplished family. His circumstances had been once splendid; they were then respectable, but he had passed through events which threatened his *all*. Those sufferings which generous souls sustain for the sake of others, not for themselves, had alone destroyed the resemblance which once existed between this excellent man and his admirable portrait, which, at the further end of the room, presented the healthy glow, and fine proportions of manly beauty. He expressed to me, in the most charming manner, his regret, that indisposition confined him to the country, and prevented him from receiving me in Paris suitable to his own wishes, and to those claims which I had upon his attentions, by the letters of introduction which I had brought to him; but added, that he should furnish me with letters to some of his friends in town, who would be happy to supply his absence, and to make Paris agreeable to me. Monsieur O— — was as good as his word.

This amiable gentleman possessed a countenance of great genius, and a mind full of intelligence.

After an elegant supper, when his lady and daughters had withdrawn, he entered into a very interesting account of his country, of the revolution, and of his flight for the salvation of himself and family. A tolerably good opinion may be formed of the devastation which have been produced by the late republican government, by the following circumstance, which Monsieur O— — assured me, on the word of a man of honour, was correct.

His section in Paris was composed of one thousand three hundred persons, of rank and fortune, of whom only five had escaped the slaughter of the guillotine!!

Madame O— — and her charming family, seemed wholly to occupy his heart and affections.

He spoke of his lady with all the tender eulogium of a young lover. Their union was entirely from attachment, and had been resisted on the part of Madame O— —, when he first addressed her, only because her fortune was humble, compared with his. He informed me, and I must not suppress the story, that in the time of blood, this amiable woman, who is remarkable for the delicacy of her mind, and for the beauty and majesty of her person, displayed a degree of coolness and courage, which, in the field of battle, would have covered the hero with laurels. One evening, a short period before the family left France, a party of those murderers, who were sent for by Robespierre, from the frontiers which divide France from Italy, and who were by that archfiend employed in all the butcheries, and massacres of Paris, entered the peaceful village of la Reine, in search of Monsieur O——. His lady saw them advancing, and anticipating their errand, had just time to give her husband intelligence of their approach, who left his chateau by a back door, and secreted himself in the house of a neighbour. Madame O——, with perfect composure, went out to meet them, and received them in the most gracious manner. They sternly demanded Mons. O——, she informed them that he had left the country, and after engaging them in conversation, she conducted them into her drawing room, and regaled them with her best wines, and made her servants attend upon them with unusual deference and ceremony. Their appearance was altogether horrible, they wore leather aprons, which were sprinkled all over with blood, they had large horse pistols in their belts, and a dirk and sabre by their sides. Their looks were full of ferocity, and they spoke a harsh dissonant patois language. Over their cups, they talked about the bloody business of that day's occupation, in the course of which they drew out their dirks, and wiped from their handles, clots of blood and hair. Madame O—— sat with them, undismayed by their frightful deportment. After drinking several bottles of Champaign and Burgundy, these savages began to grow good humoured, and seemed to be completely fascinated by the amiable and unembarrassed, and hospitable behaviour of their fair landlady. After carousing till midnight, they pressed her to retire, observing that they had been received so handsomely that they were convinced Monsieur O—— had been misrepresented, and was no enemy to the *good cause*; they added that they found the wines excellent, and after drinking two or three bottles more, they would leave the house, without causing her any reason to regret their admission.

Madame O——, with all the appearance of perfect tranquillity and confidence in their promises, wished her unwelcome visitors a good night, and after visiting her children in their rooms, she threw herself upon her bed, with a loaded pistol in each hand, and, overwhelmed with suppressed agony and agitation, she *soundly* slept till she was called by her servants, two hours after these wretches had left the house. He related also another instance of that resolution which is not unfrequently exhibited by women, when those generous affections, for which they are so justly celebrated, are menaced with danger. About the same period, two of the children of Monsieur O—— were in Paris at school: A rumour had reached him, that the teachers of the seminary in which they were placed, had offended the government, and were likely to be butchered, and that the carnage which was expected to take place, might, in its undistinguishing fury, extend to the pupils. Immediately upon receiving this intelligence, Monsieur O—— ordered his carriage, for the purpose of proceeding to town. Madame O—— implored of him to permit her to accompany him; in vain did he beseech her to remain at home; the picture of danger which he painted, only rendered her more determined. She mounted the carriage, and seated herself by the side of her husband. When they reached Paris, they were stopped in the middle of the street St. Honoré, by the massacre of a large number of prisoners who had just been taken out of a church which had been converted into a prison. Their ears were pierced with screams. Many of the miserable victims were cut down, clinging to the windows of their carriage. During the dreadful delays which they suffered in passing through this street, Madame O—— discovered no sensations of alarm, but stedfastly fixed her eyes upon the back of the coach box, to avoid, as much as possible, observing the butcheries which were perpetrating on each side of her.

Had she been observed to close her eyes, or to set back in the carriage, she would have excited a suspicion, which, no doubt, would have proved fatal to her. At length she reached the school which contained her children, where she found the rumour which they had received was without foundation; she calmly conducted them to the carriage, and during their gloomy return through Paris, betrayed no emotions; but as soon as they had passed the barrier, and were once more in safety upon the road to their peaceful chateau, the exulting mother, in an agony of joy, pressed her children to her bosom, and in a state of mind wrought up to frenzy, arrived at her own house, in convulsions of ghastly laughter. Monsieur O—— never spoke of this charming woman, without exhibiting the strongest emotions of regard. He said, that in sickness she suffered no one to attend upon him but herself, that in all his afflictions she had supported him, and that she mitigated the deep melancholy which the sufferings of his country, and his own privations, had fixed upon him, by the well-timed sallies of her elegant fancy, or by the charms of her various accomplishments.

I found myself a gainer in the article of delight, by leaving the gayest metropolis that Europe can present to a traveller, for the sake of visiting such a family.

CHAPTER XIII.

Breakfast. —Warmth of French Expression. —Rustic Eloquence. —Curious Cause assigned for the late extraordinary Frost. —Madame R— —. —Paul I. —Tivoli. —Frescati.

In the morning we breakfasted in the drawing room, in which the murderous myrmidons of Robespierre had been regaled. It was beautifully situated. Its windows looked into a grove which Monsieur O—— had formed of valuable american shrubs. His youngest daughter, a beautiful little girl of about five years of age, rather hastily entered the room with a pair of tame wood pigeons in her hands, which, in her eagerness to bring to her father, she had too forcibly pressed, who very gently told her, it was cruel to hurt her little favourites, more particularly as they were a species of bird which was remarkable for its unoffending innocence. The little creature burst into tears, "my little Harriet, why do you weep?" said her father, kissing her white forehead, and pressing her to him. "Why do you rebuke me?" said the little sufferer, "when you know I love you so much that I could kiss your naked heart."

I mention this circumstance, to show how early in life, the french children imbibe the most charming expressions, by which their more mature conversation is rendered so peculiarly captivating. During our repast, a circumstance occurred, which produced an unusual vivacity amongst all the party, and afforded a specimen of the talent and pleasantry of the french country people. The gardener entered, with the paper, and letters of the day. Amongst them, was a letter which had been opened, appeared very much disordered, and ought to have been received upon the preceding day. Monsieur O—— seemed much displeased, and called upon his man to explain the matter. The gardener, who possessed a countenance which beamed with animation and good humour, made a low bow, and without appearing to be, in the least degree, disconcerted, proceeded to unfold the affair, with the most playful ingenuity. He stated that the dairy maid was very pretty, that she made every body in love with her, and was very much in love herself, that she was accustomed to receive a great number of billet doux, which, on account of her education having been very far below her incomparable merits, she was not able to understand, without the assistance of Nicolene, the groom, who was her confident, and amanuensis; that on the day before, he gave her the letter in question, with directions to carry it to his master, that under the influence of that thoughtful absence which is said to attend the advanced stages of the tender passion, she soon afterwards conceived that it was no other than a customary homage from one of her many admirers, upon which she committed the supposed depositary of tender sighs and brittle vows, to the warm custody of her glowing bosom, than which, the gardener, (who at this moment saw his master's eyes were engaged by the *sullied* appearance of the letter) declared that nothing was fairer; he again proceeded, by observing, that in the course of the preceding evening, as she was stooping to adjust her stool in the meadow, the cow kicked, and the epistle tumbled into the milk pail; that she afterwards dried it by the kitchen fire, and gave it, for the reasons before assigned, to her confidential friend to explain to her, who soon discovered it to be a letter of business, addressed to his master, instead of an impassioned love ditty for the tender Marie; that, finally, all the principals concerned in this unhappy affair were overwhelmed with distress, on account of the sad disaster, and that the kitchen had lost all its vivacity ever since. No advocate could have pleaded more eloquently. All the family, from its chief, to little Harriet, whose tears were not yet dried, were in a continued fit of laughing. The gardener, whose face very largely partook of the gaiety which he had so successfully excited, was commissioned, by his amiable master, to tell the distressed dairy maid, that love always carried his pardon in his hand for all his offences, and that he cheerfully forgave her, but directed the gardener, to prevent a recurrence of similar accidents, not again to trust her with his letters until the tender disease was radically removed. The rustic orator gracefully bowed; and left us to finish our breakfast with increased good humour, and to carry forgiveness and consolation to poor Marie and all her condoling friends in the kitchen. Before we had completed our repast, a little deformed elderly lady made her appearance, whose religion had been shaken by the revolution, into a crazy and gloomy superstition. She had scarcely seated herself, before she began a very rapid and voluble comment upon the change of the times, and the devastations which the late extraordinary frost had committed upon the vineyards of France, which she positively asserted, with the confidence which only the arrival of her tutelar saint with the intelligence ought to have inspired, was sent as an *appropriate* judgment upon the republic, to punish it, for suffering the ladies of Paris to go so thinly clothed. Monsieur O— — heard her very patiently throughout, and then observed, that the ways of Heaven were inscrutable, that human ingenuity was baffled, in attempting to draw inferences from its visitations, and that it did not appear to him at least, that an offence which was assuredly calculated to inspire sensations of warmth and tenderness, was *appropriately* punished by a chastisement of an *opposite* tendency, to which he added, that some moralists who indulged in an endeavour to connect causes and effects, might think it rather incompatible with their notions of eternal equity, to endeavour to clothe the ladies, by stripping the land to nakedness—here the old lady could not help smiling. Her amicable adversary pursued the advantage which his pleasantry had produced, by informing her, that prognostications had been for a long period discountenanced, and that formerly when the ancient augurs, after the ceremonies of their successful illusions were over, met each other by accident in the street, impressed by the ridiculous remembrance of their impositions, they could not help laughing in each other's faces. Madame V— — laughed too; upon which Monsieur O— —, very good humouredly told her, that as a soothsayer, she certainly would not have smiled, unless she intended to retire for ever from the office. Previous to my taking leave of Monsieur O— — and his charming family, we walked in the gardens, where our conversation turned upon the extraordinary genius, who in the character of first consul of the french, unites a force, and extent of sway unknown to the kings of France, from their first appearance, to the final extinction of monarchy.

He told me that he had the honour of knowing him with intimacy from his youth, and extolled, with high eulogy, his splendid abilities, and the great services which he had rendered France. He also related several amiable anecdotes of the minister Talleyrand, who, when in

America, had lived with him a considerable time under the same roof.

At length the cabriolet, which was to bear me from this little Paradise, approached the gate, and the moment arrived when I was to part with one of the most charming families to be found in the bosom of the republic.

As Monsieur O— — pressed me by one hand, and placed that of his little Harriet in my other, a tear of exquisite tenderness rolled down his cheek, it seemed to express that we should never meet again on this side the grave. Excellent being! if it must be so, if wasting and unsparing sickness is destined to tear thee ere long from those who delight thine eye, and soothe thine heart in the midst of its sorrows, may the angel of peace smile upon thee in thy last moments, and bear thy mild and generous, and patient spirit, to the realms of eternal repose! Adieu! dear family of la Reine.

Upon my return to Paris, I proceeded to the hotel of Monsieur R— —. Curiosity led me to view the house, and the celebrated bed of his lady, who was then in London.

The little vanities and eccentricities of this elegant and hospitable woman, will find immediate forgiveness, when it is known that she is now very young, and was married, when a spoiled child of the age of fourteen, to her present husband. She is one of David's most enthusiastic admirers, and has carried the rage for grecian undress, to an extremity, which, even in the capital, left her without a follower.

In the public walks of the Champs Elysées, she one evening presented herself in a dress which almost rivalled the robes of Paradise; the parisians, who are remarkable for their politeness to women, and are not remarkable for scrupulous sentiments of delicacy, were so displeased with her appearance, that they made a lane to the entrance for her, and expelled the modern Eve from the Elysian Fields, not with a "flaming sword of wrath," but with hisses softly uttered, and by gentle tokens of polite disapprobation. She tells her friends, that her cabinet is crowded with letters of the most impassioned love, from persons of the first fame, distinction, and opulence. In her parties, when conversation begins to pause, she introduces some of these melting epistles, which she is said to read with a bewitching pathos, and never fails to close the fond recital by expressions of the tenderest pity for the sufferings of their ill-starred authors. She has declared, that some of her lovers equal the Belvidere Apollo in beauty, but that she never has yet seen that being, who was perfect enough to be entitled to the possession of her affections. Do not smile. Madame R is a disciple of Diana, even slander pays incessant homage to her chastity. Rumour has whispered, in every corner of Paris, that her husband is only admitted to the honour of supplying the finances of her splendid and costly establishment. Madame R— — has not yet produced any of the beautiful and eloquent arguments of Cornelia, to disprove the strange assertion. Her chamber, which constitutes one of the sights of Paris, and which, after what has been just mentioned, may be justly considered, in or out of France, as a great curiosity, is fitted up in a style of considerable taste, and even magnificence. The bed upon which this charming statue reposes, is a superb sofa, raised upon a pedestal, the ascent to which is by a flight of cedar steps, on each side are altars, on which are placed Herculaneum vases of flowers, and a large antique lamp of gold; the back of the bed is formed by an immense pier glass, and the curtains, which are of the most costly muslin, festooned with golden tassels, descend in beautiful drapery from a floral crown of gold. It is said that the late emperor of Russia, after the laborious and successful diplomatic intrigues of messrs. Talleyrand and Sieyes, and a certain lady, became enamoured, by description, with the immaculate goddess of Mont Blanc, and that he sent confidential commissioners to Paris, to report her daily dress, and to order copies of her furniture.

The story may be believed, when the hero of it was well known to be fully qualified for one of the deepest dungeons of a madhouse. I hope, for the sake of society, and the repose of the world, that the rest of Madame R— —'s admirers have not united to their passion the bewildered imagination, which fatally distinguished, and finally closed the career of her imperial lover.

Mr. R— — is very polite to the english, and his letters ensure the greatest attention wherever they are produced.

From Mont Blanc I proceeded to the Hotel de Caramand, the residence of the british ambassador, to whom I had a letter of introduction, from a particular friend of his, and who received me with great politeness. His apartments were handsome, and looked into some beautiful gardens. Amongst the english, who were at this time in Paris, a little prejudice existed against the representative of the british monarch, from a reason, which within the jurisdiction of the lord mayor of London and of most corporate towns in England, will be considered to carry considerable weight. The envoy did not celebrate the late birthday of his sovereign by a jolly, and convivial dinner. The fact was, Mr. M— —, who by the sudden return of Mr. J— —, became unexpectedly invested with the dignity of an ambassador, was in constant expectation of being recalled, to make room for the intended appointment of lord W— — to the consular court, in consequence of which, he had not prepared for the display of those splendid hospitalities, which, on such occasions, always distinguish the table of a british house of embassy.

On a Sunday evening, I went with a party to Tivoli, a favourite place of amusement with the parisians. At the entrance we found, as at all the public places, a guard of horse, and foot. The admission is twenty sols. The evening was very fine. We passed immense crowds of people, who were flocking to the same place. Amongst them were many elegant, well dressed women, wholly unattended by gentlemen, a circumstance by no means unusual in Paris. This place seemed to be raised by the magic touch of enchantment. We entered upon gravelled walks, which were cut through little winding, and intersecting hillocks of box; those which formed the sides were surmounted by orange trees, which presented a beautiful colonnade; immediately after we had passed them, we entered an elegant treillage of honeysuckles, roses, and eglantine, which formed the grand entrance to the garden. Here a most animated scene of festivity opened upon us. On one side were rope dancers, people riding at the ring, groups of persons playing at shuttlecock, which seemed to be the favourite, and I may add, the most ridiculous diversion; on the other side, were dancers, tumblers, mountebanks, and parties, all with gay countenances, seated in little bowers enjoying lemonade, and ices. In the centre as we advanced, were about three hundred people, who were dancing the favourite waltz. This dance was brought from Germany, where, *from its nature*, the partners are always engaged lovers; but the french, who think that nothing can be blamable which is susceptible of elegance, have introduced the german dance, without adhering to the german regulation. The attitudes of the waltz are very graceful, but they would not altogether accord with english female notions of delicacy. At a late fashionable parisian ball, a gentleman present was requested by the lady of the house, to waltz with a friend of hers, who was without a partner. The person of this neglected fair, was a little inclined to the meagre. The gallant, without the least embarrassment, declined, observing, "Ah! ma chere Madame qu'exigez vous de moi, ne savez vous pas qu'elle n'a point de sein?" In the middle of the platform of the dancers, a very fine full band was playing. At the end of this raised stage, a very capacious indian marquee was erected, which was beautifully illuminated with variegated lamps, and under its broad canopy, a large concourse of people was seated, some were enjoying conversation, some were playing at buillotte, drinking coffee, &c.; behind this building, was a noble corinthian temple, from the doors of which, were covered trellis walks, leading to spacious gardens, which were formed to display the different tastes of the english, french, and dutch nations, whose respective names they bore. These gardens are intersected by little canals, upon which several persons were amusing themselves with the diversion of canoe racing. The whole was illuminated by large patent reflecting lamps, which shed a lustre almost as brilliant as the day. A few english were present, amongst them were the duchess of Cumberland, and a few other ladies. These gardens, previous to the revolution, were the property of a wealthy minister of France, who, it is said, expended near one hundred thousand pounds sterling, in bringing them to perfection, which he just saw accomplished, when he closed his eyes upon the scaffold. The nation became their next proprietor, who sold them for a large sum of money to their present owners.

From this place we went to Frescati, which is the promenade of the first beauty, and fashion of Paris, who generally assemble about half past ten o'clock, after the opera is concluded. No admission money is required, but singular as it may seem, no improper intruder has yet appeared, a circumstance which may be accounted for by the awe which well bred society ever maintains over vulgarity. Frescati is situated in the Italian Boulevard; was formerly the residence of a nobleman of large fortune, and has also undergone the usual transition of revolutionary confiscation. The streets leading to it were filled with carriages. After ascending a flight of steps, from a handsome court yard, we entered a beautiful hall, which was lined with pier glasses, and decorated with festoons of artificial flowers, at the end of it was a fine statue of Venus de Medicis. On one side of this image was an arch, which led into a suite of six magnificent apartments, which were superbly gilt, painted, and also covered with pier glasses, and lustres of fine diamond cut glass, which latter, looked like so many little glittering cascades. Each room was in a blaze of light, and filled with parties, who were taking ices, or drinking coffee. Each room communicated with the others, by arches, or folding doors of mirrors. The garden is small, but very tastefully disposed. It is composed of three walks, which are lined with orange and acacia trees, and vases of roses. At the end is a tower mounted on a rock, temples, and rustic bridges; and on each side of the walks, are little labyrinth bowers. On the side next to the Boulevard, is a terrace which commands the whole scene, is lined on each side with beautiful vases of flowers, and is terminated at each end by alcoves, which are lined with mirrors. Here in the course of an hour, the astonished, and admiring stranger may see near three thousand females of the first beauty and distinction in Paris, whose cheeks are no longer disfigured by the corrosion of rouge, and who, by their symmetry and grace, would induce him to believe, that the loveliest figures of Greece, in her proudest era, were revived, and moving before him.

CHAPTER XIV.

Convent of blue Nuns. — Duchesse de Biron. — The bloody Key. — Courts of Justice. — Public Library. — Gobelines. — Miss Linwood. — Garden of Plants. — French Accommodation. — Boot Cleaners. — Cat and Dog Shearers. — Monsieur S— — and Family.

The english convent, or as it is called, the convent of blue nuns, in the Rue de St. Victoire, is the only establishment of the kind, which throughout the republic, has survived the revolution. To what cause its exclusive protection is attributable, is not, I believe correctly known. But though this spot of sacred seclusion, has escaped the final stroke of extermination, it has sustained an ample share of the general desolation. During the time of terrour, it was converted into the crowded prison of the female nobility, who were here confined, and afterwards dragged from its cloisters, and butchered by the guillotine, or the daggers of assassins. I had a letter of introduction to Mrs. S— —, one of the sisterhood, a lady of distinguished family in England. I found her in the refectory. A dignified dejection overspread her countenance, and her figure seemed much emaciated by the scenes of horrour through which she had passed. She informed me, that when the nuns were in a state of arrestation by the order of Robespierre, the convent was so crowded with prisoners, that they were obliged to eat their wretched meals in three different divisions. The places of the unhappy beings who were led off to execution, were immediately filled by fresh victims.

Amongst those who suffered, was the beautiful young duchesse de Biron, said to be one of the loveliest women of the french court. Her fate was singular, and horrible. One morning, two of the assistant executioners came into one of the rooms, and called upon the female citizen Biron to come forward, meaning the old duchesse de Biron, the mother, who was here immured with her daughter; some one said, which of them do you require? The hell-hounds replied, "Our order was for one only, but as there are two, we will have both, that there may be no errour." The mother and daughter were taken away, locked senseless in each others arms. When the cart which carried them arrived at the foot of the scaffold, the chief executioner looked at his paper, which contained a list of his victims, and saw the name of only one Biron; the assistants informed him that they found two of that name in the convent, and to prevent mistake, they had brought both. The principal, with perfect sang froid, said it was all well, wrote with a pencil the article "les" before the name Biron, to which he added an s, and immediately beheaded both!!!

Mrs. S—— led me to the chapel, to show me the havoc which the unspairing impious hands of the revolution had there produced. She put into my hand an immense massy key to open the door of the choir. "That key," said she, "was made for the master-key of the convent, by the order of Robespierre. In the time of terrour, our gaoler wore it at his belt. A thousand times has my soul sunk within me, when it loudly pushed the bolt of the lock aside. When the door opened, it was either a signal to prepare for instant death to some of those who were within, or for the gloomy purpose of admitting new victims." When we entered the chapel, my surprise and abhorrence were equally excited. The windows were beaten through, the hangings were flapping in the wind, the altar was shattered in pieces and prostrate, the pavement was every where torn up, and the caves of the dead were still yawning upon us. From their solemn and hallowed depths, the mouldering relics of the departed had been raised, by torch light, and heaped in frightful piles of unfinished decay against the walls, for the purpose of converting the lead, which contained these wretched fragments of mortality, into balls for the musketry of the revolution. The gardens behind the chapel must have been once very pleasant, but they then had the appearance of a wilderness. The painful uncertainty of many years, had occasioned the neglect and ruin in which I saw them. Some of the nuns were reading upon shattered seats, under overgrown bowers, and others were walking in the melancholy shade of neglected avenues. The effect of the whole was gloomy and sorrowful, and fully confirmed the melancholy recital which I received from Mrs. S——. Bonaparte, it is said, intends to confirm to these nuns their present residence, by an act of government.

Upon leaving the convent I visited the seats of cassation, and justice, in the architectural arrangement of which, I saw but little worthy of minute notice, except the perfect accommodation which pervades all the french buildings, which are appropriated to the administration of the laws.

The hall of the first cassation, or grand court of appeal, is very fine. The judges wear elegant costumes, and were, as well as the advocates, seated upon chairs, which were constructed to imitate the seats of roman magistracy, and had a good effect. I was informed that the whole of the ornamental arrangement was designed by David.

From the courts of justice, I went to the second national library, which is very noble and large, and has a valuable collection of books. Several students were arranged with great silence and decorum, at long tables. In one apartment is a very large, and ingenious model of Rome in a glass case, and another of a frigate.

Upon leaving the library I proceeded to the Gobelins, so called from one Gobel, a noted dyer at Rheims, who settled here in the reign of Francis I. This beautiful manufactory has a crowd of visitors every day. Upon the walls of the galleries the tapestry is suspended, which exhibits very exquisite copies of various historical paintings, of which there are some very costly and beautiful specimens. The artists work behind the frame, where the original from which they copy is placed. The whole is a very expensive national establishment, much of its production is preserved for presents to foreign princes, and some of it is disposed of by public sale.

Upon the comparison between the works of the Gobelins and the beautiful works of Miss Linwood, I could not help feeling a little degree of pride to observe that my ingenious countrywoman did not appear to suffer by it. Too much praise cannot be bestowed upon the tasteful paintings of her exquisite needle. This elegant minded woman has manifested by her charming exhibition, that great genius is not always separated from great labour, and unwearied perseverance.

From the Gobelins I visited the garden of plants, which is considered to be the largest, and most valuable botanical collection in Europe, and was founded by the celebrated Buffon. The garden is laid out into noble walks, and beds containing the rarest plants from all parts of the world, each of which is neatly labelled for the use of the students. On the right of the entrance is a park containing all sorts of deer, and on the left are vast hothouses and greenhouses; in the centre, enclosed in iron lattice work, is a large pond for the reception of foreign aquatic animals, very near which is a large octagon experimental beehive, about ten feet high, and at the end, near the banks of the Seine, is a fine menagerie, in which, amongst other beasts, there are some noble lions. Many of the animals have separate houses, and gardens to range in. Adjoining is the park of the elephant. This stupendous animal, from the ample space in which he moves, is seen to great advantage, and is considered to be the largest of his species in Europe. Near the entrance, on the right, is the museum of natural curiosities, the collection of which is very valuable, and admirably arranged. There is here a fine giraffe, or camelopard, of an amazing height, stuffed. This surprising animal is a native of Ethiopia, and some other parts of Africa, and has scarcely ever been seen in Europe.

From the garden of plants, I made all possible dispatch to Madame C— —'s, in the Boulevard Italien, where I was engaged to dinner.

Upon crossing the Pont Neuf, where there are a number of little stalls erected, the owners of which advertise upon little boards, which are raised upon poles, that they possess extraordinary talents for shearing dogs and cats; I could not help stopping and laughing most heartily to observe the following address to the public from one of these canine and grimalkin functionaries:

"Monin, tondit et coupe
les chiens la chatte
et sa femme— —
vat en ville."

Which runs in this ridiculous manner in english:

"Monin shears and cuts
dogs and cats and his wife — —
goes on errands."

As I had no time to return to my hotel to dress, I was initiated into a mode of expeditiously equipping myself, by a young friend who was with me, to which I was before a stranger, and which shows in the most trifling matters, that the french are good adepts in expedition and accommodation. In passing through the Palais Royal, we entered the little shop of a boot cleaner. In a moment I was mounted upon a dirty sopha, to which I ascended by steps, and from which I had a complete commanding view of the concourse of gay people, who are always passing and repassing in this idle place; the paper of the day, stretched upon a little wooden frame was placed in my hand, each foot was fixed upon an iron anvil, one man brushed off the dirt, and another put on a shining blacking, a third brushed my clothes, and a fourth presented a basin of water and towel to me. The whole of this comfortable operation lasted about four minutes. My dirty valets made me a low bow for four sols, which, poor as the recompense was, exceeded their expectations by three pieces of that petty coin.

In the evening, I had the happiness of being introduced to Monsieur S— —. Under his noble and hospitable roof, amidst his affectionate, beautiful, and accomplished family, and in the select circle of his elegant and enlightened society, I passed many happy hours. Monsieur S— — was of a noble family, and previous to the revolution was one of the fermiers generaux, and possessed a very noble fortune. In discharging the duties of his distinguished and lucrative office, he conciliated the affections of every one, who had the good fortune to be comprehended within the compass of his honourable authority, and when the revolution stripped him of it, it found his integrity without a stain, except what, in the bewildered interpretation of republican fury, adhered to him from his connection with the old established order of things. In the general, and undistinguishing cry for blood, which yelled from the remorseless assassins of Robespierre, this admirable man was consigned to a dungeon, and doomed to the scaffold. Two hours before he was to suffer, the remembrance of the noble victim, and of a series of favours, of kindness, and of generosity, flashed, with momentary but irresistible compunction, upon the mind of one of his sanguinary judges, who, suspending the bloody proceedings which then occupied the court, implored the compassion of his fell associates. He pleaded until he had obtained his discharge, and then at once forgetting the emotions of mercy, which had inspired his tongue with the most persuasive eloquence, he very composedly resumed the functions of his cruel occupation, and consigned to the fatal instrument of revolutionary slaughter, other beings, whose virtues were less renowned, or less fortunate in their sphere of operation. Monsieur S— — had reached his sixty-eighth year, but seemed to possess all the vivacity and health of youth. His lady was a very amiable, and enlightened woman. Their family consisted of a son, and three daughters, all of them handsome, and very highly accomplished. The eldest, Madame E— —, excelled in music; the second, Madame B— —, in poetry and the classics; and the youngest, Mademoiselle Delphine, in drawing and singing. I shall, perhaps, be pardoned for introducing a little impromptu compliment, which the pure, and unassuming merits of the youngest of the family, drew from my pen, in consequence of the conversation one evening, turning upon the indecorum of the tunic dress, amongst the elegantes of Paris.

TO MADEMOISELLE D.S.

Whilst art array'd in tunic robe,
Tries over fashion's gaudy globe,
To hold resistless force,
Thy merits shall impede her course,
For grace and nature gain in thee,
A chaste, decisive victory.

From the general wreck of property Monsieur S— — has been fortunate enough to save a considerable portion of his former fortune. A similar favourable circumstance has, in general, rewarded the fortitude and constancy of those who, in the political storm, refused to seek a dastard safety by flight. Influenced by the

reputation of the integrity, talents, and experience of Monsieur S——
, the first consul has deservedly placed him at the head of the
national accounts, which he manages with great advantage, and
honour to the government. I was pressed to make this charming
house my home. Upon a noble terrace, which communicated with
the drawing room, and commanded a view of all the gayety, and
fashion of the Italien Boulevard, which moved below us, in the circle
of some of the most charming people of Paris, we used to enjoy the
refreshing coolness of the evening, the graceful unpremeditated
dance, or the sounds of enchanting music. In this happy spot all
parties assembled. Those who had been divided by the ferocity of
politics, here met in amiable intercourse. I have in the same room
observed, the once pursuing republican conqueror, in social converse
with the captive vendeean general, who had submitted to his
prowess, and to the government. The sword was not merely
sheathed—it was *concealed* in flowers. To please, and to be pleased;
to charm, and to enlighten, by interchanges of pleasantry, and
politeness, and talents, and acquirements, seemed alone to occupy
the generous minds of this charming society. The remembrance of
the hours which I passed under this roof, will afford my mind
delight, as long as the faculty of memory remains, or until high
honour, and munificent hospitality have lost their value, and genius
and beauty, purity and elegance have no longer any attractions.

CHAPTER XV.

Civility of a Sentinel. — The Hall of the Legislative Assembly. — British House of Commons. — Captain Bergevet. — The Temple. — Sir Sydney Smith's Escape. — Colonel Phillipeaux.

One morning, as I was entering the grand court of the hall of the Legislative Assembly, I was stopped by a sentry. I told him I was an Englishman. He politely begged my pardon, and requested me to pass, and called one of the housekeepers to show me the apartments.

This magnificent pile is in the Fauxbourg St. Germain, and was formerly the palace of the Bourbons. After passing through a suite of splendid apartments, I entered, through lofty folding doors, into the hall, where the legislators assemble. It is a very spacious semicircular room, and much resembles, in its arrangements the appearance of a splendid theatre before the stage. The ascent to the seat of the president is by a flight of light marble steps; the facing of his bureau is composed of the most costly marble, richly carved. On each side of the president's chair are seats for the secretaries; and immediately below them is the tribune, into which the orator ascends to address the House. On each side of the seat of the president are antique statues of eminent patriots and orators, which are placed in niches in the wall. Under the tribune, upon the centre of the floor, is the altar of the country, upon which, in marble, is represented the book of the laws, resting upon branches of olive. Behind it, upon semicircular seats, the legislators sit, at the back of whom are the boxes of the embassadors, and officers of state, and immediately above them, within a colonnade of corinthian pillars, the public are admitted. Round the upper part of the cornice, a beautiful festoon of lilac coloured cloth, looped up with rich tassels, is suspended, for the purpose of correcting the vibration of the voice. The whole is very superb, and has cost the nation an immense sum of money. The principal housekeeper asked me "whether our speakers had such a place to declaim in," I told him, "that we had very *great* orators in England, but that they were content to speak in very little places."

He laughed, and observed, "that frenchmen never talked to so much advantage as when their eye was pleased."

This man I found had been formerly one of the door keepers of the national assembly, and was present when, after having been impeached by Billaud, Panis, and their colleagues, Tallien discharged his pistol at Robespierre, whom he helped to support, until the monster was finally dispatched by the guillotine, on the memorable 9th of Thermidor.

The french are amazingly fond of finery and stage effect. The solicitude which always first manifested itself after any political change in the course of the revolution, was the external decoration of each new puppet who, arrayed in the brief authority of the fleeting moment, was permitted to "play his fantastic tricks before high Heaven."

The poor battered ark of government was left overturned, under the protection of an escort of assassins, in the ensanguined mud, upon the reeking bodies of its former, headless, bearers, until its new supporters had adjusted the rival pretensions of silk and satin, and had consulted the pattern book of the laceman in the choice of their embroidery. On one side of the arch which leads into the antiroom of the legislative assembly, are suspended patterns and designs for tickets of admission to the sitting, elegantly framed, and near the same place, in a long gallery which leads to the dressing-rooms of the legislators, are boxes which contain the senatorial robes of the members. The meetings of our house of commons would inspire more awe, and veneration, if more attention was paid to decorum, and external decoration. A dignified and manly magnificence would not be unsuitable to the proceedings of the sanctuary of british laws, and the seat of unrivalled eloquence. What would a perfumed french legislator say, accustomed to rise in the rustling of embroidered silks, and gracefully holding in his hand, a cap of soft and showy plumes, to address himself to alabaster statues, glittering lustres, grecian chairs, festoons of drapery, and an audience of beings tricked out as fine as himself, were he to be suddenly transported into a poor and paltry room, meanly lighted, badly ventilated, and inconveniently arranged, and to be told that, in that spot, the representatives of the first nation in the world, legislated for her subjects? What would he say, were he to see and hear in the mean attire of jockeys and mechanics, such orators as Greece and Rome never saw or heard in the days of their most exalted glory; unfolding with the penetration of a subordinate Providence, the machinations of a dark and deep conspiracy, erecting elaborate laws to shelter the good, against the enemies of repose, or hurling the thunder of their eloquence against the common foes of their country. The astonished frenchman would very likely say, "I always thought that the english were a strange set of beings, but they now exceed the powers of my comprehension, they can elicit wit in the midst of gloom, and can say such things in a plain unbrushed coat of *blue* cloth, as all the robes, plumes, and finery of the republic, in her gaudy halls of deliberation, cannot inspire."

From the legislative assembly I went to pay my respects to the gallant captain Bergeret, to whom I had letters of introduction. It will be immediately remembered, that this distinguished hero, in the Virginie, displayed the most undaunted courage, when she was engaged by sir Edward Pellew, in the Indefatigable, to whose superior prowess and naval knowledge, he was obliged to strike the tricolour flag. His bravery and integrity have justly entitled him to the admiration and lasting friendship of his noble conqueror, and to the esteem of the british nation. When sir Sidney Smith was confined in the Temple, and captain Bergeret a prisoner in England, the latter was sent to France upon his parole, to endeavour to effect the exchange of sir Sidney. The french government, which was then under the direction of some of the basest and meanest of her tyrants, refused to listen to the proposal; and at the same time resisted the return of their own countryman.

The gallant Bergeret was resolved to preserve his word of honour unsullied, or to perish in the attempt. Finding all his efforts to obtain the liberation of the illustrious captive unavailing, menaced with death if he departed, and invited by promised command and promotion if he remained, he contrived to quit his own country by stealth, and returned a voluntary exile to his generous and confiding conquerors.

From captain B——'s hotel I went to the Temple, so celebrated in the gloomy history of the revolution. It stands in the Rue du Temple, in the Fauxbourg of that name. The entrance is handsome, and does not much impress the idea of the approach to a place of such confinement. Over the gates is a pole, supporting a dirty and tattered bonnet rouge, of which species of republican decoration there are very few now to be seen in Paris. The door was opened to me by the principal gaoler, whose predecessor had been dismissed on account of his imputed connivance in the escape of sir Sidney Smith. His appearance seemed fully to qualify him for his savage office, and to insure his superiors against all future apprehension, of a remission of duty by any act of humanity, feeling, or commiseration. He told me, that he could not permit me to advance beyond the lodge, on account of a peremptory order which he had just received from government. From this place I had a full command of the walk and prison, the latter of which is situated in the centre of the walls. He pointed out to me the window of the room in which the royal sufferers languished. As the story of sir Sidney Smith's escape from this prison has been involved in some ambiguity, a short recital of it will, perhaps, not prove uninteresting.

After several months had rolled away, since the gates of his prison had first closed upon the british hero, he observed that a lady who lived in an upper apartment on the opposite side of the street, seemed frequently to look towards that part of the prison in which he was confined. As often as he observed her, he played some tender air upon his flute, by which, and by imitating every motion which she made, he at length succeeded in fixing her attention upon him, and had the happiness of remarking that she occasionally observed him with a glass. One morning when he saw that she was looking attentively upon him in this manner, he tore a blank leaf from an old mass book which was lying in his cell, and with the soot of the chimney, contrived, by his finger, to describe upon it, in a large character, the letter A, which he held to the window to be viewed by his fair sympathizing observer. After gazing upon it for some little time, she nodded, to show that she understood what he meant, sir Sidney then touched the top of the first bar of the grating of his window, which he wished her to consider as the representative of the letter A, the second B, and so on, until he had formed, from the top of the bars, a corresponding number of letters; and by touching the middle, and bottom parts of them, upon a line with each other, he easily, after having inculcated the first impression of his wishes, completed a telegraphic alphabet. The process of communication was, from its nature, very slow, but sir Sidney had the happiness of observing, upon forming the first word, that this excellent being, who beamed before him like a guardian angel, seemed completely to comprehend it, which she expressed by an assenting movement of the head. Frequently obliged to desist from this tacit and tedious intercourse, from the dread of exciting the curiosity of the gaolers, or his fellow prisoners, who were permitted to walk before his window, sir Sidney occupied several days in communicating to his unknown friend, his name and quality, and imploring her to procure some unsuspected royalist of consequence and address sufficient for the undertaking, to effect his escape; in the achievement of which he assured her, upon his word of honour, that whatever cost might be incurred, would be amply reimbursed, and that the bounty and gratitude of his country would nobly remunerate those who had the talent, and bravery to accomplish it. By the same means he enabled her to draw confidential and accredited bills, for considerable sums of money, for the promotion of the scheme, which she applied with the most perfect integrity. Colonel Phelipeaux was at this time at Paris; a military man of rank, and a secret royalist, most devoutly attached to the fortunes of the exiled family of France, and to those who supported their cause. He had been long endeavouring to bring to maturity, a plan for facilitating their restoration, but which the loyal adherent, from a series of untoward and uncontrollable circumstances, began to despair of accomplishing. The lovely deliverer of sir Sidney, applied to this distinguished character, to whom she was known, and stated the singular correspondence which had taken place between herself and the heroic captive in the Temple. Phelipeaux, who was acquainted with the fame of sir Sidney, and chagrined at the failure of his former favourite scheme, embraced the present project with a sort of prophetic enthusiasm, by which he hoped to restore, to the british nation, one of her greatest heroes, who, by his skill and valour, might once more impress the common enemy with dismay, augment the glory of his country, and cover himself with the laurels of future victory. Intelligent, active, cool, daring, and insinuating, colonel Phelipeaux immediately applied himself to bring to maturity, a plan at once suitable to his genius, and interesting to his wishes. To those whom it was necessary to employ upon the occasion, he contrived to unite one of the clerks of the minister of the police, who forged his signature with exact imitation, to an order for removing the body of sir Sidney, from the Temple to the prison of the Conciergerie: after this was accomplished, on the day after that on which the inspector of gaols was to visit the Temple and Conciergerie, a ceremony, which is performed once a month in Paris, two gentlemen of tried courage and address, who were previously instructed by colonel Phelipeaux, disguised as officers of the marechaussee, presented themselves in a fiacre at the Temple, and demanded the delivery of sir Sidney, at the same time showing the forged order for his removal. This the gaoler attentively perused and examined, as well as the minister's signature. Soon after the register of the prison informed sir Sidney of the order of the directory, upon hearing which, he at first appeared to be a little disconcerted, upon which the pseudoofficers gave him every assurance of the honour and mild intentions of the government towards him, sir Sidney seemed more reconciled, packed up his clothes, took leave of his fellow prisoners, and distributed little tokens of his gratitude to those servants of the prison, from whom he had experienced indulgencies. Upon the eve of their departure, the register observed, that four of the prison guard should accompany them. This arrangement menaced the whole plan with immediate dissolution. The officers, without betraying the least emotion, acquiesced in the propriety of the measure, and gave orders for the men to be called out, when, as if recollecting the rank and honour of their illustrious prisoner, one of them addressed sir Sidney, by saying, "citizen, you are a brave officer, give us your parole, and there is no occasion for an escort." Sir Sidney replied, that he would pledge his faith, as an officer, to accompany them, without resistance, wherever they chose to conduct him.

Not a look or movement betrayed the intention of the party. Every thing was cool, well-timed, and natural. They entered a fiacre, which, as is usual, was brought for the purpose of removing him, in which he found changes of clothes, false passports, and money. The coach moved with an accustomed pace, to the Faubourg St. Germain, where they alighted, and parted in different directions. Sir Sidney met colonel Phelipeaux at the appointed spot of rendezvous.

The project was so ably planned and conducted, that no one but the party concerned was acquainted with the escape, until near a month had elapsed, when the inspector paid his next periodical visit. What pen can describe the sensations of two such men as sir Sidney and Phelipeaux, when they first beheld each other in safety? Heaven befriended the generous and gallant exploit. Sir Sidney and his noble friend, reached the french coast wholly unsuspected, and committing themselves to their God, and to the protective genius of brave men, put to sea in an open boat, and were soon afterwards discovered by an english cruising frigate, and brought in safety to the british shores.

The gallant Phelipeaux soon afterwards accompanied sir Sidney in the Tigre to Acre, where, overwhelmed by the fatigue of that extraordinary campaign, in which he supported a distinguished part, and the noxious influence of a sultry climate, operating upon a delicate frame, he expired in the arms of his illustrious friend, who attended him to his grave, and shed the tears of gratitude and friendship over his honoured and lamented obsequies. But ere the dying Phelipeaux closed his eyes, he received the rewards of his generous enterprise. He beheld the repulsed legions of the republic, flying before the british banners, and the irresistible prowess of his valiant companion; he beheld the distinguished being, whom he had thus rescued from a dungeon, and impending destruction, by an act of almost romantic heroism, covered with the unparticipated glory, of having overpowered a leader, who, renowned, and long accustomed to conquest, saw, for the first time, his *invincible troops* give way; who, inflamed to desperation, deemed the perilous exposure of his person necessary, to rally them to the contest, over bridges of their slaughtered comrades, but who at length was obliged to retire from the field of battle, and to leave to the heroic sir Sidney, the exclusive exultation of announcing to his grateful and elated country, that he had fought, and vanquished the laurelled conqueror of Italy, and the bold invader of Egypt.

Sir Sidney has no vices to conceal behind his spreading and imperishable laurels. His public character is before the approving world. That peace which his sword has accelerated, has afforded us an undisturbed opportunity of admiring his achievements in the field, and of contemplating his conduct in the retired avenues of private life, in which his deportment is without a stain. In him there is every thing to applaud, and nothing to forgive.

Yet thus glorious in public, and thus unsullied in private, the conqueror of Bonaparte, and the saviour of the east, owes the honours, *which he adorns*, to foreign and distant powers.

To the *grateful* government of his own country, he is indebted for an ungracious paltry annuity, inadequate to the display of ordinary consequence, and wholly unequal to the suitable support of that dignity, which ought for ever to distinguish such a being from the mass of mankind.

The enemies of sir Sidney, for envy furnishes every great man with his quota of such indirect eulogists, if they should honour these pages with a perusal, may, perchance, endeavour to trace the approving warmth with which I have spoken of him, to the enthusiasm of a friendship dazzled, and undiscriminating; but I beg to assure them, that the fame of sir Sidney is better known to me than his person, and that his noble qualities have alone excited the humble tribute which is here offered to one, for whom delighted Nature, in the language of our immortal bard,

"— — — — — — — — — — — —might stand up,
and say to all the world, this *is* a man— —"

CHAPTER XVI.

A fashionable Poem. — Frere Richart. — Religion. — Hôtel des Invalides. — Hall of Victory. — Enemies' Colours. — Sulky Appearance of an English Jack and Ensign. — Indecorum. — The aged Captain. — Military School. — Champ de Mars. — The Garden of Mousseaux.

The conversation whilst I was at Paris, was much engaged by a poem, describing the genius and progress of christianity written in imitation of the style of Ossian, which excited very considerable curiosity. From the remarks of some shrewd acquaintances of mine, who had perused the work, I learnt that the principles of the poem seemed strongly tinctured with the bewildered fancies of a disordered mind, conveyed in very heavy *prosaic* blank verse. "It was the madness of poetry, without the inspiration."

This composition may be considered as a curiosity, from other reasons than those which mere criticism affords. The poem was bad, the readers were many. The subject was sacred, the author a reputed atheist, and the profits which it produced exceeded two thousand pounds sterling. The fortunate writer relieved himself from the jaws of famine by this strange incomprehensible eulogy on the charms and advancement of christianity, which has been received in Paris, with a sort of fashionable frenzy. Another pseudobard has announced his intention very shortly of issuing from the press, a work which he conceives will be more saleable and a greater favourite with the public, in which he intends ironically to combat the doctrine of the Trinity, by gravely resembling it to the Deity taking snuff between two looking glasses, so that when he sneezes, two resemblances of him are seen to sneeze also, and yet that there are not three sneezers, but one sneezer.

Some other outlines of this work were imparted to me at Paris, but the pen turns with disgust and detestation, from such low and nauseous profanation. I have only condescended to mention the composition, and the last anecdote, to show how much the world is deluded, by the received opinion that the french are become a new race of exemplary devotees. The recoil from atheism to enthusiasm, is not unusual, but the french in general have not, as yet, experienced this change. That they are susceptible of extraordinary transitions, their history and revolution have sufficiently manifested. In the Journal de Paris, written in the reigns of Charles VI and VII, is preserved rather a curious account of the velocity with which religious zeal has, in former periods, been excited. "On the 4th day of April, 1429," says the journal, "the duke of Burgundy came to Paris, with a very fine body of knights and esquires; and eight days afterwards there came to Paris, a cordelier, by name Frere Richart, a man of great prudence, very knowing in prayer, a giver of good doctrine to edify his neighbour, and was so successful, that he who had not seen him, was bursting with envy against those who had. He was but one day in Paris, without preaching. He began his sermon about five o'clock in the morning, and continued preaching till ten or eleven o'clock, and there were always between five and six thousand persons to hear him preach. This cordelier preached on St. Mark's Day, attended by the like number of persons, and on their return from his sermon, the people of Paris were so turned, and moved to devotion, that in three or four hours time, there were more than one hundred fires lighted, in which they burnt their chess boards, their back gammon tables, and their packs of cards."

To this sort of fanaticism, the parisians are unquestionably not arrived. A more eloquent man than the Frere Richart, must appear amongst them, before such meliorations as are recorded in the Paris journal, can be effected in the dissolute and uncontrolled habits of that gay and voluptuous city. I do not mean, from any previous remark which I have made, to infer that there are not many good and very pious people in France, and it has been a favourable circumstance to the ancient religion of the country, that the revolution never attempted any reform in it, or to substitute another mode of worship. That great political change in the ebullition of its fury, prostrated the altars of the old church, without raising others of a new, or improved construction. It presented a hideous rebellion against the glorious author of all good, and declared an indiscriminate war of extermination against his ministers and followers, and every principle of the Gospel and morality. Every form of faith, every mode of adoration, fell indiscriminately under the proscriptions of its unsparing wrath. The towering abbey and humble oratory, were alike swept away in the general tornado, and mingled their ruins together. But the race of the good were not all expelled from this scene of havoc and outrage. The voice of piety still found a passage to her God. The silent prayer pierced through the compact covering of the dungeon, and ascended to Heaven. Within the embowering unsearchable recesses of the soul, far beyond the reach of revolutionary persecution, the pure unappalled spirit of devotion erected her viewless temple, in secret magnificence, sublime, and unassailable!

The child who had never heard the bell of the sabbath sound, who had never beheld the solemn ceremonies of authorized adoration, was told that those awful and splendid piles, which filled his eyes with wonder, and his mind with instinctive reverence, were raised for other purposes than those of becoming auxiliary to the ferocity of war. That genius and taste, and toil and cost, had not thus expended their unrivalled powers, and lavished their munificent resources, in erecting *gothic* magazines of gunpowder, and *saxon* sheds for the accommodation of atheistic fabricators of revolutionary cannon balls.

The young observer in private, and by stealth imbibed, from parental precept or example, the sentiment of a national religion, suppressed, not extinguished, or in the gloomy absence of all indications of it, remained unsolicited by any rival mode of worship to bestow his apostacy upon an alien creed. Thus the minds of the rising generation, who were engaged in favour of the catholic persuasion, during the frightful period of its long denunciation, by stolen, secluded and unfinished displays of its spirit and form, contemplated its return with animated elation, or beheld its approach, unimpressed with those doubts or prejudices which religious, as well as secular competitions, very frequently excite; in that auspicious hour, when the policy, if not the piety of a powerful government, restored it to the French people. The subject is highly interesting; but I must resign it to abler pens for more ample discussion.

I was much gratified by being presented to the celebrated philosopher Mons. Charles, by Madame S——. He has a suite of noble apartments in the Louvre, which have been bestowed upon him by the government, as a grateful reward for his having presented to the nation his magnificent collection of philosophical apparatus. He has also, in consideration of his ability and experience, been constituted the principal lecturer on philosophy. In these rooms his valuable and costly donation is arranged. In the centre of the dome of the first apartment, called the Hall of Electricity, is suspended the car of the first balloon which was inflated with inflammable air, in which he and his brother ascended in the afternoon of the 1st of December, 1783, in which they continued in the air for an hour and three quarters; and after they had descended, Mons. C—— rose alone to the astonishing height of 10,500 feet. In the same room are immense electrical machines and batteries, some of which had been presented to him by Madame S——.

In this room, amongst many other fanciful figures, which are used for the purpose of enlivening the solemnity of a philosophical lecture by exciting sentiments of innocent gayety, was a little Cupid. The tiny god, with his arrow in his hand, was insulated upon a throne of glass, and was charged with that electric fluid which not a little resembles the subtle spirit of his nature. The youngest daughter of Madame S——, who accompanied us, was requested to touch it. In a moment it discharged its penetrating spark—"Oh! how that little god has alarmed me!" said the recoiling fair one, whose youthful countenance surprise had imbued with new beauties; "but yet," said she, recovering herself, *"he does not hurt."* This little sally may be considered as a specimen of that playful sprightliness which is so much the characteristic of the french female.

In the centre of another room, dedicated to optics, as we entered, we saw a beautiful nosegay in a vase, which appeared to be composed of the rarest flowers. I approached it with an intention of inhaling its fragrance, when, lo! my hand passed through it. It was an exquisite optical illusion. "Ah!" said my elegant and moralising companion, Madame S——, smiling, "of such flowers has Happiness composed *her* wreath: it is thus she gladdens with it the eye of Hope; but the hand of Expectation can never grasp it."

The graceful moral deserves a more lasting record than it will find in these few and perishable pages.

In the other rooms are all sorts of apparatus for trying experiments in the various branches of that department of science, over which Mons. C—— so ably presides.

The merit of Mons. C—— has no rival but in his modesty. Considering the rank and estimation which he bears in the republic, his external appearance is singularly unassuming. I have been with him in the gardens of the Thuilleries, when they were thronged with the fashion and gayety of Paris, where he has appeared in a suit of plain brown cloth, an old round hat with a little national cockade in it, under which he presented a countenance full of character, talent and animation. In this homely puritan garb, he excited more respectful curiosity, wherever he moved, than some generals who paraded before us in dresses upon which the tailor and embroiderer had long laboured, and who added to their stature by laced hats entirely filled with gaudy buoyant plumes.

From Mons. Charles we went to the church of St. Rocque, in the Rue St. Honorè. As we entered, the effect of a fine painting of our Saviour crucified, upon which the sun was shining with great glory, placed at the extremity of the church, and seen through several lessening arches of faint, increasing shade, was very grand. This church has been more than once the scene of revolutionary carnage. Its elegant front is much disfigured, and the doors are perforated, in a great number of places, by the ball of cannon and the shot of musketry. Mass was performing in the church; but we saw only few worshippers, and those were chiefly old women and little girls.

From St. Rocque we proceeded to the Hôtel des Invalides, the chapel and dome of which are so justly celebrated. The front is inferior to the military hospital at Chelsea, to which it bears some resemblance. The chapel is converted into the Hall of Victory, in which, with great taste, are suspended, under descriptive medallions, the banners of the enemies of the republic, which have been taken during the late war, the numbers of which are immense. The same decoration adorns the pilasters and gallery of the vast, magnificent dome at the end of the hall.

My eye was naturally occupied, immediately after we had entered, in searching amongst the most *battered* of the banners, for the british colours: at last I discovered the jack and ensign of an english man of war, pierced with shot-holes, and blackened with smoke, looking very sulky, and indignantly, amongst the finery, and tawdry tatters of italian and turkish standards.

In the course of this pursuit, I caught the intelligent eye of Madame S——. She immediately assigned to my search the proper motive. "Ah!" said she, laughingly, and patting me on the arm with her fan, "we are, as you see, my dear Englishman, very vain; and you are very proud."

A stranger to the late calamitous war, unable to marshal in his mind the enemies of the republic, might here, with a glance of his eye, whilst contemplating this poor result of devastation, enumerate the foes of France, and appreciate the facilities or difficulties of the victory.

In observing, amidst this gaudy show of captive colours, only two hardworn banners of their rival enemy, he would draw a conclusion too flattering and familiar to an English ear, to render it necessary to be recorded here.

Upon the shattered standards of Austria he would confer the meed of merited applause for heroic, although unprevailing bravery.

To the banners of Prussia he would say, "I know not whether principle or policy, or treachery, or corruption, deterred you from the field—Your looks exhibit no proofs of sincere resistance—However, you never belonged to cowards."

The neapolitan ensign might excite such sentiments as these: "You appear for a short time to have faced the battle—You were unfortunate, and soon retired."

To the gaudy drapeaus of the italian and turkish legions, which every where present the appearance of belonging to the wardrobe of a pantomimic hero, he would observe, "The scent of the battle has not perfumed you; its smoke has not sullied your shining, silky sides. Ye appear in numbers, but display no marks of having waved before a brave, united and energetic band."

In this manner might he trace the various fate of the war. Upon several of the staffs only two or three shreds of colours are to be seen adhering. These are chiefly Austrian. On each side of the chapel are large, and some of them valuable paintings, by the french masters, representing the conquests of the french armies at different eras.

It is a matter not unworthy of observation, that although the revolution with a keen, and savage eye, explored too successfully, almost every vestige of a royal tendency, the beautiful pavement under the dome of the invalides has escaped destruction. The fleur de lis, surmounted by the crown of France, still retains its original place, in this elegant and costly marble flooring. The statues of the saints have been removed; and their places are supplied by the new order of revolutionary deities; but the names of the ancient figures have not been erased from the pedestals of the new ones: to which omission the spectator is indebted for a smile when contemplating the statue of Equality, he reads, immediately below his feet, "*St. Louis.*"

There is here a costly monument erected to the memory of the brave marshal Turenne, who was killed by a cannon ball in 1675. In my humble opinion, it is too much in the false taste of french statuary. A groupe of weeping angels surround the recumbent hero, in the attitudes of operatic figurantes, in whose faces, and forms, the artist has attempted, too laboriously and artificially, to delineate the expressions of graceful grief. On each side of the vast arch which divides the dome from the chapel, are raised the tablets of military honour, on which, in characters of gold, the names of those soldiers are recorded who have distinguished themselves for their achievements in the late war. As we were contemplating a painting upon a very large scale, in which, amongst other figures, is an uncovered whole length of a warrior, a prudish-looking lady, who seemed to have touched the age of desperation, after having very attentively beheld it with her glass for some time, observed to her party, that there was a great deal of indecorum in the picture. Madame S—— very shrewdly whispered in my ear, that the indecorum was in the remark.

When we were just leaving the chapel, we overheard a sun-browned soldier, who had lost both his legs, observe to his companion, to whom he was explaining the colours, pointing to the banners of the turkish cavalry, the tops of whose staffs were surmounted with horses' tails, "Look at those ribbands; they are not worthy of being worn when won." This military hospital is capable of accommodating 3,000 soldiers. The bedrooms, kitchens, refectory and outoffices are very capacious, and, what is rather unusual in France, clean and comfortable. The day before we were there, the first consul paid a visit to its veteran inhabitants. Amongst them, he recognised an old, and very brave soldier, whose exploits were the frequent theme of his aged comrades. The young general told him that he should die a captain, took him in his carriage to dine with him at Mal Maison, presented him with a medallion of honour, and conferred upon him the rank of a captain, in one of the most distinguished regiments.

From this place we went to the military school adjoining, in which Bonaparte received the rudiments of that education which was destined to form the foundation of his future glory. The building is large and handsome, and is, from a very natural sentiment, in high favour with the first consul. There is nothing in it particular to describe. The grounds and gardens are very spacious and fine. In the front of the military school is the celebrated Champ de Mars, which is an immense flat space of ground. On each side are rising terraces of earth, and double rows of trees; and at the further end, the river Seine flows. On days of great national celebrations, this vast plain is surrounded with Gobelins tapestry, statues, and triumphal arches. After contemplating these objects of public curiosity, we returned to Mons. S— — to dinner, where we met a large party of very pleasant people. Amongst them I was pleased with meeting a near relative of an able and upright minister of the republic, to whose unwearied labours the world is not a little indebted for the enjoyments of its present repose.

After dinner we drove to the beautiful garden of Mousseau, formerly the property of the duc d'Orleans. It is laid out with great taste, and delights the eye with the most romantic specimens of improved rural beauty. It was originally designed by its detestable owner for other purposes than those of affording to a vast and crowded city the innocent delights and recreations of retired and tasteful scenery. In the gloom of its groves, all sorts of horrible profanations were practised by this monster and his midnight crew, at the head of whom was Legendre the Butcher. Every rank recess of prostitute pollution in Paris was ransacked to furnish materials for the celebration of their impure and impious orgies. The ode to Atheism, and the song of Blasphemy, were succeeded by the applauding yells of Drunkenness and Obscenity.

At the time we visited this garden it belonged to the nation, and was open, on certain days, to well-dressed people. A few days afterwards, it was presented, as a mark of national esteem, to Cambaceres, the second consul.

Here we rambled till the evening. The sun was setting. The nightingales were singing in great numbers. Not a cloud to be seen. A breeze, blowing through a plantation of roses, refreshed us with its coolness and fragrance. In a sequestered part of this beautiful ground, under the embowering shades of Acacia trees, upon the ruins of a little temple, we seated ourselves, and were regaled by some charming italian duets, which were sung by Madame S— — and her lovely daughter, with the most enchanting pathos. I hope I shall be pardoned for introducing some lines which were written upon our return, by an enthusiastic admirer of merit and music.

TO MADEMOISELLE D. S——.

In Mousseau's sweet arcadian dale,
   Fair Delphine pours the plaintive strain;
She charms the list'ning nightingale,
   And seems th' enchantress of the plain.

Blest be those lips, to music dear!
   Sweet songstress! never may they move
But with such sounds to soothe the ear,
   And melt the yielding heart to love!

May sorrow never bid them pour
   From the torn heart one suffering sigh,
But be thy life a fragrant flow'r,
   Blooming beneath a cloudless sky.

CHAPTER XVII.

Curious Method of raising Hay. — Lucien Bonaparte's Hôtel. — Opera. — Consular Box. — Madame Bonaparte's Box. — Feydeau Theatre. — Belle Vue. — Versailles. — The Palace of the Petit Trianon. — The Grounds.

The people of Paris, who keep horses in stables at the back of their houses, have a singular mode of keeping their hay in the lofts of their dwelling houses. At the top of a spacious and elegant hotel, is to be seen a projecting crane in the act of raising loads of winter provision for the stable. When I first saw this strange process, my surprise would scarcely have been increased, had I beheld the horse ascending after the hay.

I must not forget to offer some little description of the opera, where, during my stay, through the politeness of Madame H——, I had free access to a private box.

This spacious and splendid theatre is lighted from above by an immense circular lustre of patent lamps. The form of this brilliant light is in the antique taste, and it is said to have cost two thousand pounds sterling. The effect which it produces in the body of the theatre, and upon the scenery, is admirable. It prevents the sight from being divided, and distracted by girandoles. This establishment is upon so vast a scale, that government, which is the proprietor, is always a loser upon balancing the receipts and disbursements of each night. The stage and its machinery have for many years occupied a great number of the subordinate classes of people, who, if not employed in this manner, would in all probability become burdensome, and unpleasant to the government. To this circumstance is attributable the superiority of the machinery, and scenery, over every other theatre which I ever saw. In the english theatres, my eye has often been offended at the representations of the internal parts of houses, in which not a chair, or table is introduced, for the purpose of carrying on the ingenious deception. Upon the stage of the french opera, every scene has its appropriate furniture, and distinctive appendages, which are always produced as soon as the scene drops, by numerous attendants. From this attention to the minute circumstances of the drama, the illusion becomes enchanting. The orchestra is very fine, and is composed of ninety eminent musicians. The corps de ballet consists of between eighty and ninety fine dancers, of whom Monsieur Deshayes is the principal. His movements are more graceful, his agility more surprising, and his step more light, firm, and elastic, than those of any dancer whom I have ever seen. He is very justly considered to be the first in Europe. The first consul has a private box here, on one side of which, a lofty, hollow, decorative column rises, the flutes of which are open, and through which he views, [printing unclear: unseen,] the audience and performers. The beholder might be almost inclined to think that this surprising man had borrowed from our immortal bard, his notions of exciting the impression of dignity, by a rare, and well timed display of his person.

"Thus did I keep my person fresh, and new;
My presence like a robe pontifical,
Ne'er seen but wondered at: and so my state
Seldom, but sumptuous shewed, like a feast
And won by rareness such solemnity."

Madame Bonaparte's box is on the left side of the stage, over the door, in which the hapless queen has frequently displayed her beautiful person to the enraptured audience.

The Feydeau theatre is very elegant; and on account of its excellent arrangements, good performers, and exquisite machinery, is much resorted to, and is in general preferred to the fourteen other dramatic spectacles which, in this dissipated city, almost every night present their tribute of pleasure to the gay, and delighted parisians. A frenchman once observed to me, that a Sunday in London was horrible, on account of there being no playhouses open at night! The decorum and good manners which are even still observed in all the french places of public amusement, are very impressive, and agreeable. Horse and foot soldiers are stationed at the avenues, to keep them clear, to prevent depredation, and to quell the first indications of popular commotion.

I was much gratified by an excursion to Versailles, which had been some time planned by the charming family of the S— —'s. We set off early in the morning, in one of the government carriages, and after a delightful ride, through a very rich, and luxuriant country, of about twelve miles, the vast, and magnificent palace of Versailles, opened upon our view, at the end of a street nearly two miles long, lined on each side with noble hotels, and gardens. It was on a Sunday, the day on which the palace is opened to the public. On the road, we passed several hundreds of persons in carriages, cabrioles, or walking; all with merry faces, in showy clothes, and adorned with bouquets, on their route to this spot of favourite delight.

About four miles from Paris we saw Belle Vue, formerly the residence of Mesdames; soon afterwards we passed the noble palace, and park of St. Cloud, which was preparing for the reception of the first consul.

At the entrance of the village of St. Cloud, on the left, after we had passed the bridge, we saw a very pretty house, and grounds, belonging to a tanner, who had amassed considerable wealth by a discovery of tanning leather in twenty-four hours, so as to render it fit for the currier. Whether he possesses this faculty or not, I cannot from my own experience say, but I can venture to affirm, that the leather of France is very bad. In the village is a very noble porcelain manufactory, which unfortunately we had not time to inspect.

Whilst our horses were refreshing themselves with a little water, we were beset by the agents of the different hotels, and restaurateurs of Versailles, who presented us with little cards, announcing in a very pompous manner the superiority of their employers accommodations.

The stables of Versailles, to the right, and left, are from the designs of Mansart, in the form of a crescent, and have the appearance of princely residences. Here the late King kept in the greatest style six hundred of the finest horses. On the left of the grand gateway, is a military lodge for the accommodation of cavalry. It represents in shape, an immense turkish marquee. After we had passed the pallisades of the first court, we more distinctly saw this amazing pile of irregular buildings, which consists of the old castle, the new palaces, the houses of the ministers of state, and servants, two opera houses, the chapel, military schools, museums, and the manufactory of arms, the whole of which are now consolidated, and form one palace.

The beautiful pavement of black and white marble in the court yards, is much defaced, and their fountains are totally destroyed.

The first place we visited was the manufactory of small arms; the resident workmen in which exceed two thousand men. Here we saw all the ingenious process of constructing the musket, pistol, and sabre, of which there are an immense collection; and also several carbines, and swords of honour, intended as presents from the first consul to officers and soldiers of distinguished merit.

From the manufactory of small arms, we returned to the grand court, and entered a suite of rooms, which contain the relics of the former valuable cabinet of curiosities. Several of those which we saw, were worthy of attention. From these rooms, we passed to the late king's private opera house, which surpasses in magnificence, and costly decoration, every thing of the kind I ever beheld. The facing of the whole of the inside is of carved wood, richly gilt. The dome is beautifully painted. Upon the scenery of the stage being removed, and temporary columns, and galleries raised; all of which can be effected in twenty-four hours, that part of the theatre presents a counterpart of the other, and the whole forms a most splendid oblong ball room, very deservedly considered to be the finest in Europe: it used to be illuminated by ten thousand wax lights. The concert rooms, and retiring apartments are also very beautiful. From the opera, we visited the chapel, which is very fine, and costly, in which there are many large, and valuable paintings. After leaving this deserted place of royal worship, we passed through the Halls of Plenty, Venus, Mars, Mercury, Apollo, and the Hall of the Billiard Table, finely painted by Houasse, le Brun, Champagne, and other eminent artists, to the grand gallery, which is seventy-two yards long, and fourteen broad, and has seventeen lofty windows on one side, which look into the gardens, and seventeen immense pier glasses on the opposite side to correspond. In this gallery, the kings of France were accustomed to receive ambassadors, and ministers of state.

We next entered the bedroom of the late queen and beheld the door, which, on the night of the 6th of October, 1789, the frantic, and sanguinary mob, headed by the infamous Legendre, burst open, for the purpose of dispatching her with daggers, in her bed, on that frightful night, which preceded the return of the royal family to Paris, under the protection of the marquis de la Fayette, through an enraged multitude, which extended itself from Versailles to Paris.

The miserable queen saved herself by escaping into an adjoining apartment. Her bed was pierced through and through with poignards. The door is nailed up, but the marks of that horrible outrage still remain. In this, and in the adjoining chambers, are some very beautiful and valuable paintings. I must not omit to mention, although the sentiment which it inspires is not very pleasant, the representation of the capture of an english frigate, by la Bayonne, a french corvette, after a desperate engagement, in which victory for once decided in favour of the enemy, who opposed, on this occasion, an inferior force. This is a picture of infinite merit, and possesses a novelty of arrangement, and strength of colouring, which I never saw equalled in any other naval representation. The subject seldom admits of much variety. The french, of course, are very much pleased with it. There are here also some curious old clocks.

It was in one of these apartments, that Prior, the celebrated poet, when secretary to the earl of Portland, who was appointed ambassador to the french court, in the year 1698, made the following memorable answer.

One of the french king's household was showing the bard the royal apartments and curiosities of this palace, and particularly pointed out to his notice, the paintings of le Brun, now removed to the museum of the arts, in which the victories of Lewis the XIVth are described, and asked him, whether the actions of king William were to be seen in his palace? No, sir, replied the loyal wit, "the monuments of my master's glory are to be seen every where but in his own house."

Through the interest of Monsieur S—— we were admitted into a private room below stairs, in which several portraits of the late royal family have been preserved from destruction, during the late revolution. That which represents the queen and her young family, is very fine, and displays all the bewitching beauty and vivacity of that lovely and unfortunate personage. Into this room no one was admitted with us. Here is a very curious piece of mechanism: it is a painting, containing two hundred little figures, in the act of enjoying the various pleasures of rural sport, which are separated from the back ground of the picture, and are set in motion by springs; and admirably imitate all the movements natural to their different occupations. A fisherman throws in his line, and draws up a little fish, a regular chase is displayed, and a nuptial procession appears, in which little figures, riding in tiny carriages, nod to the spectators. There are also many other curious figures. It is glazed and framed, and at a distance, when its motion has ceased, it has the appearance of a tolerably good painting. We next quitted the palace, and entered upon the grand terrace, from which it makes the finest appearance.

This enormous pile of building is here united by a centre, and corresponding wings, of great extent and magnificence.

From this elevated spot, the beholder contemplates the different waterworks, walks, and gardens, which cover several miles.

The orangery is a beautiful specimen of tuscan architecture, designed by le Maitre, and finished by Mansart. It is filled with lofty orange trees in full bearing; many of which, in their tubs, measure from twenty to thirty feet high. Amongst them is an orange tree which is upwards of four hundred years old. The cascades, fountains, and jets d'eau, are too numerous to admit of minute description. They are all very fine, and are supplied by prodigious engines across the Seine, at Marli, about three miles distant. The Trianon is a little marble palace, of much beauty, and embellished with the richest decoration.

It stands at the end of the great lake, in front of the palace; and was, by its late royal owners, considered as a summer house to the gardens of Versailles. The whole of this vast building and its grounds, were improved and beautified by Lewis XIVth, for the well known purpose of impressing his subjects, and particularly his courtiers, with the highest opinion of his greatness, and the lowest of their comparative littleness. Amongst the lords of his court he easily effected his wishes, by accommodating them in a manner unsuitable to their dignity.

Ruins of the Queen's Farm-house in the Petit Trianon.

After being astonished at such a display of gorgeous magnificence, I approached, with increased delight, the enchanting little palace and grounds of the late queen, distant from Versailles about two miles, called the Petit Trianon, to which she very justly gave the appellation of her "little Palace of Taste." Here, fatigued with the splendours of royalty, she threw aside all its appearances, and gave herself up to the elegant pleasures of rural life. It is a princely establishment in miniature. It consists of a small palace, a chapel, an opera house, out offices and stables, a little park, and pleasure grounds; the latter of which are still charming, although the fascinating eye, and tasteful hand of their lovely but too volatile mistress, no longer pervade, cherish and direct their growth and beauty. By that reverse of fortune, which the revolution has familiarized, the Petit Trianon is let out by the government to a restaurateur. All the rooms but one in this house were preoccupied, on the day of our visit, in consequence of which we were obliged to dine in the former little bed room of the queen, where, like the idalian goddess, she used to sleep in a suspended basket of roses. The apertures in the ceiling and wainscot, to which the elegant furniture of this little room of repose had once adhered, are still visible.

After dinner we hastened through our coffee, and proceeded to the gardens. After winding through gravelled walks, embowered by the most exquisite and costly shrubs, we entered the elegant temple of Cupid, from which the little favourite of mankind had been unwillingly, and rudely expelled, as appeared by the fragments of his pedestal.

Thy wrongs little god! shall be revenged by thy fair friend Pity. Those who treated thee thus, shall suffer in their turn, and she shall not console them!

From this temple we passed through the most romantic avenues, to a range of rural buildings, called the queen's farm, the dairy, the mill, and the woodmens cottages; which, during the queen's residence at the Petit Trianon, were occupied by the most elegant and accomplished young noblemen of the court. In front of them, a lake terminated on one side by a rustic tower, spreads itself. These buildings are much neglected, and are falling into rapid ruin.

In other times, when neatness and order reigned throughout this elysian scenery, and gracefully spread its luxuriant beauties at the feet of its former captivating owner, upon the mirror of that lake, now filled with reeds and sedges, in elegant little pleasure boats, the illustrious party was accustomed to enjoy the freshness of the evening, to fill the surrounding groves with the melody of the song, which was faintly answered by the tender flute, whose musician was concealed in that rustic tower, whose graceful base the honeysuckle and eglantine no longer encircle, and whose winding access, once decorated with flowers of the richest beauty and perfume, is now overgrown with moss, decayed, and falling piecemeal to the ground.

Near the farm, in corresponding pleasure grounds, the miller's house particularly impressed us with delight. All its characteristics were elegantly observed. A rivulet still runs on one side of it, which formerly used to turn a little wheel to complete the illusion. The apartments, which must have been once enchanting, now present nothing but gaping beams, broken ceilings, and shattered casements. The wainscots of its little cabinets, exhibit only a tablet, upon which are rudely penciled, the motley initials, love verses, and memorandums of its various visitors.

The shade of the ivy, which, upon all occasions, seems destined to perform the last offices to the departing monuments of human ingenuity, has here exercised its gloomy function. Whilst we were roving about, we were obliged to take refuge from a thunder storm, in what appeared to us a mere barn; upon our entering it, we found it to be an elegant little ball room, much disfigured, and greened over by damp and neglect. In other parts of this *petit Paradis*, are caves of artificial rock, which have been formed at an immense expense, in which were formerly beds of moss, and through which clear streams of water glided, Belvidere temples, and scattered cottages, each differing from its neighbour in character, but all according in taste and beauty. The opera house, which stands alone, is a miniature of the splendid one in the palace of Versailles.

The sylvan ball room, is an oblong square, lined with beautiful treillages, surmounted with vases of flowers. The top is open. When the queen gave her balls here, the ground was covered by a temporary flooring, and the whole was brilliantly lighted. As we passed by the palace, we saw, in the queen's little library, several persons walking.

Could the enchanting beauty of Austria, and the once incensed idol of the gay, and the gallant, arise from her untimely tomb, and behold her most sacred recesses of delight, thus rudely exposed, and converted into scenes of low, and holiday festivity, the temples which she designed, defaced, their statues overthrown, her walks overgrown and entangled, the clear mirror of the winding lake, upon the placid surface of which once shone the reflected form of the

Belvidere, and the retreats of elegant taste covered with the reedy greenness of the standing pool, and all the *fairy fabric* of her graceful fancy, thus dissolving in decay; the devoted hapless Marie would add another sigh to the many which her aching heart has already heaved!

It would be a very desirable thing if Bonaparte would make this his country palace instead of St. Cloud. Upon our return, as we approached Paris, the illuminated bridges of the Seine looked very beautiful, and we were much pleased with some fireworks, which had a singular effect upon the water.

In the evening, we had some music at Monsieur S——'s, where we were joined by general Marescot, a brave and distinguished officer, much esteemed by Bonaparte. He informed us that he was on the point of setting out to view and report the condition of all the maritime fortifications in the republic. "You must go with me as my aide-de-camp," said the general to Mademoiselle D——. "I am not fierce enough for a soldier," replied the fair one, with a bewitching smile. "Well then," observed the sun-browned general, "should the war ever be renewed, you shall attend me to charm away its calamities."

Madame S——, like a true french mother, was delighted with the little compliment, and presenting her snuff box to the gallant Marescot, she said, "thank you, my dear general, the brave always think generously of the fair."

CHAPTER XVIII.

Bonaparte's Talents in Finance. — Garrick and the Madman. — Palace of the Conservative Senate. — Process of transferring Oil Paintings from Wood to Canvas. — The Dinner Knife. — Commodités. — Hall of the National Convention. — The Minister Talleyrand's Levee.

The first consul is said to add to his other extraordinary powers, an acute and comprehensive knowledge of finance. Monsieur S—— informed me, that whenever he waited upon him in his official capacity, with the national accounts, he displayed an acquaintance with the most complicated statements, which seemed intuitive.

He exhibits the same talents in philosophy, and in matters which are foreign to those vast objects of public employ, which have raised him to his present height of glory, and which in general preclude the subordinate enjoyment of elegant study.

Those acquirements, which providence in its wisdom has thinly scattered amongst mankind, and which seldom ripen to full maturity, although cherished by the most propitious advantages, and by the unreposing labours of a long, and blissful existence, spread their rich abundance, in the May morning of life, before this extraordinary being, who in the commencement of that very revolution, upon the ruins of which he has stepped to supreme authority, was a beardless stripling.

From the great performers upon the public stage of life, our conversation, one evening, at Madame S——'s, by a natural transition, embraced a review of the wonderful talents, which have at various times adorned the lesser drama of the theatre. Madame S—— made some judicious remarks upon the french players of distinction, to all of whom she imputed a manner, and enunciation which have been imbibed in a school, in which nature has not been permitted to preside. Their tragedy, she said, was inflated with too much pomp, and their elegant comedy suffered by too volatile an airiness. She bestowed upon our immortal Garrick, the most decided preference, and superiority to any actor whom she had ever seen. The opportunity which she had of judging of his powers, was short, and singular, but fully enabled her to form a decisive opinion. When Garrick visited Paris for the last time, she was just married. This celebrated actor had letters of introduction to Monsieur S——. At a large party, which Monsieur S—— formed for the purpose of doing honour to his distinguished visitor, he exhibited several specimens of his unrivalled talents. Amongst others, he represented in dumb show, by the wonderful powers of his expressive countenance, the feelings of a father, who in looking over a lofty balcony with his only child in his arms, by accident dropped it. The disaster drove the unhappy parent mad. Garrick had visited him in his cell; where the miserable maniac was accustomed, several times in the course of the day, to exhibit all those looks and attitudes which he had displayed at the balcony[9]. On a sudden he would bend himself forward, as if looking from a window into the street, with his arms folded as if they embraced a child, then he would start back, and appear as if he had lost something, search the room round and round, run again forward, as to the railing of a window, look down, and beat his forehead, as if he had beheld his infant bleeding, and breathless upon the pavement. Garrick's imitation was exquisite. The feelings of his beholders were wrought up to horror. The tears, and consternation of a gay fashionable french party, were applauses more flattering to the british Roscius, than the thunder of that acclamation, which, in the crowded theatre, followed the flash of his fiery eye, or the close of his appalling speech.

The english drama, however, has not escaped the animadversions of a french critic, whose taste and liberality are not very congenial with those of my charming, and generous friend. "Their tragedies," he says, (speaking of the english) "it is true, though interesting, and replete with beauties, are nevertheless dramatic monsters, half *butchery*, and half *farce*. Grotesque characters, and extravagant pleasantry constitute the chief part of their comedies. In one of them, (not named) the devil enters sneezing, and somebody says to the devil, *God bless you*. They are not, however, all of this stamp. They have *even some* in very good taste."

Yes, Monsieur Dourx, I agree with you, I think we have *some* in very good taste. I know not in what dramatic work the facetious frenchman has discovered the introduction of his satanic majesty under the influence of a cold, and receiving, as he enters, the usual deprecation on such occasions. I rather suspect that the adventures of Punch, and his fickle lady, who are always attended by a dancing demon, have afforded the materials for this sapient observation.

In the course of one of my morning rambles in Paris, I visited the ruins of the celebrated Bastille, of which prison, only the arsenal, some fragments of its massy walls, and two or three dungeons remain. The volcanic vengeance of the people, has swept away this mighty fabric, which the revolting mind of republican liberty denounced as the frightful den of despotism, upon the approach to which no marks of returning footsteps were imprinted, whilst, in her mad career, she converted every private dwelling in the metropolis into a revolutionary prison: So much for popular consistency!

In the mutations of time, to what different purposes are the same places applied! Where the consuming martyr expired[10], the unwieldy prize hog is exposed to sale; and the modern parisian derives the sources of warmth and comfort, from a place, the very name of which, once *chilled* the circulation of his blood. The site of the Bastille is now a magazine of wood, which supplies the city with fuel.

Every lover of pure liberty must leap with delight upon the disincumbered earth, where once stood that gloomy abode of "broken hearts," and reflect upon the sufferings of the wretched Latude, and the various victims of capricious pique, or prostitute resentment. It was here that, in the beautiful lines of Cowper, the hopeless prisoner was doomed

> "To fly for refuge from distracting thought
> To such amusements as ingenious woe
> Contrives, hard shifting, and without her tools —
> To read, engraven on the mouldy walls,
> In stagg'ring types, his predecessor's tale,

143

A sad memorial, and subjoin his own —
To turn purveyor to an overgorg'd
And bloated spider, till the pamper'd pest
Is made familiar, watches his approach,
Comes at his call, and serves him for a friend —"

The cells of the Bastille were constantly filled, during the syren reign of la Pompadour over the gloomy affections of Lewis the XVth.

The overthrow of this dungeon has not rendered state prisons out of fashion in the republic, although it has mitigated the severity of their internal government. The towers of the Temple, look down upon the prostrate ruins of the Bastille.

From this memorable spot of ground, I went to the Observatory. In the rooms, which open upon an artificial terrace, were some prodigious astronomical apparatus. A very ingenious frame was then constructing, for elevating, or depressing the astronomer, and the telescope at the same time, by an easy, and simple process of machinery. The Observatory is a noble building, and contains libraries, students rooms, and apartments for the various artificers, and machinists who are occupied in fabricating the apparatus, and instruments necessary to the science of astronomy. From the exterior of the dome, there is a fine view of the city, suburbs, and country.

From the Observatory, I visited the Conservative Senate, formerly the Palace of the Luxembourg. The back of this beautiful building is in the Rue de Vaugirand, in the Fauxbourg of St. Germains. The gardens of this noble pile, are receiving great improvement, and alteration, from designs which have been approved of by the first consul, who in his wise policy, intends that they shall, in time, rival those of the Thuilleries, for the purpose of affording an elegant, and fashionable promenade to the people who reside in this part of the capital, who are considerably removed from the beautiful walks which adorn the consular palace. Here I saw the Hall of Deliberation, in which the Conservative Senate assembles. It is nothing more than a large, handsome drawing-room, in which are placed, upon rising platforms, sixty armed chairs, for so many members, the chair of the president, and the tribune. This magnificent palace is repairing, and fitting up for the residence, and accommodation of its members. I was introduced to the artist who has the care of the gallery here, and who, with his assistants, was very busily occupied in a process for removing the oil colours of a painting from wood, and transferring them to canvas. He received me with great politeness, and explained to me the mode of doing it, in which there appeared to be more toil, nicety, and steadiness required, than ingenuity.

The painting is laid upon a cloth stretched upon a marble slab, and the wood behind is shaved off until nothing but the picture, like a flat cake, or rather a sheet of goldbeater's skin, remains, a piece of canvas coated with a cement is then placed upon it, to which it adheres, and presents all the appearance of having been originally painted upon it. The pictures from the subject of St. Bruno, were then undergoing this operation.

The apartments in which these people were at work, presented very convincing indications of the mutability of human ambition.

This palace was allotted to the celebrated Council of Five Hundred. During their ephemeral reign, these very rooms were designed for their halls of audience, and levees, the rich mouldings, and cornices of which were half gilt, and covered with silver paper to preserve them: the poor council were never indulged in a house warming.

The pictures, which were collected by Henry IV, and deposited in the gallery there, which bears his name, are said to be valuable. I did not see them, on account of their having been removed into store rooms during the repairs of the palace.

It was late when I left the Luxembourg, and somewhat exhausted for want of refreshment, I determined upon dining at the first restaurateur's which I could meet with, instead of going to the Gardens of the Thuilleries. To find such an accommodation in Paris, is no difficult thing. A stranger would naturally suppose, from the frequency with which the words caffé, limonade, and restaurateur present themselves to the eye, that three parts of the inhabitants had turned their talents to the valuable study of relieving the cravings of an empty stomach.

I had not moved three yards down the Rue de Tournon, before, on my left, I saw the welcome board which, in large golden characters, announced the very best entertainment within. At this moment, the celebrated picture of the banquet in the Louvre, could scarcely have afforded me more delight. I had an excellent dinner, wine, and fruit for four livres. In the course of my repast, I begged that a knife, might be permitted to aid the services of a three pronged silver fork, which graced my plate on the left. After rather a laborious search, my wishes were gratified by an instrument, which certainly was entitled to the name of one, but was assuredly not the handsomest of its species. Whether there had been any dispute between the handle, and the blade, I know not, but there were very evident appearances of an approaching separation. Not wishing to augment the rupture, between two personages so necessary to each others service, and to those who were to be benefitted by it, I begged of my fair hostess, who, with two pretty girls (her daughters), were picking the stalks from some strawberries, which were intended for my desert, at the other end of the room, that she would favour me with another knife. The maitresse d'hôtel, who had a pair of fine dark expressive eyes, very archly said, "Why would you wish to change it, Sir? it is an english one." It certainly looked like one; no compliment could be neater. Whether I gave it too great a latitude of interpretation, I will not pretend to say, but it led me into such a train of happy *comparative thinking*, that I ate my dinner with it very comfortably, without saying another word. I have since thought, that the maitresse d'hôtel had not another knife in her house, but what was in use.

In France, I have before had occasion to remark, that fanciful notions of excessive delicacy, are not permitted to interfere with comfort, and convenience. Amongst these people, every thing turns upon the principle of accommodation. To this motive I attribute the frequent exhibition, over the doors of respectable looking houses, in the fashionable walks, and in different parts of Paris, of the following characters, "Commodités pour Hommes, et Femmes." An english prude would start to read these words. I mention this circumstance, for the purpose of communicating some idea of the people, convinced, as I well am, that it is only by detail, that we can become acquainted with the peculiar characteristics of any community.

I very often passed by the ci-devant Hall of the National Convention; in which the hapless king and queen were doomed to the scaffold, where murder was legitimated, religion denounced, and the grave declared to be the bed of *eternal repose.*

In vindication of the ways of eternal justice, even upon earth, this polluted pile is participating the fate of its devoted members.

Those walls which once resounded with the florid, high toned declamation of republican visionaries, the most worthless, imposing, and desperate of mankind, are prevented, for a short time, by a few crazy props, from covering the earth below with their dust and ruins. The famed temple of the Goddess of Liberty, is not tenantable enough to cover the Babel Deity from the peltings of the midnight storm.

Where is now the enthusiastic Gironde, where the volcanic mountain, the fiery, and eloquent Mirabeau, the wily Brissot, the atheistic Lequinios, the remorseless Marat, the bloody St. Just, and the chief of the deplumed and fallen legions of equality? All is desolate and silent. The gaping planks of the guillotine are imbued with their last traces. The haunt of the banditti is uncovered. The revolution has preyed upon her own children, and metaphysical murderers have perished by the daggers of speculative republicans.

About two years since this place was converted into a ménagerie. The cave, and the wilderness, the desert, and the jungle, presented to the eye of the beholder, representative successors of those savages who, with more powers and more ferocity, were once enclosed within the same den. From the remembrance of such miscreants, I turn, with increased satisfaction, to the traces of approaching civilization, which mark the career of the present government, in which the want of suitable splendour no longer repels the approach and friendship of those nations which once shuddered at the idea of coming into contact with the infected rags of visionary fraternity. Some indications of this change I saw pourtrayed at the levee of Monsieur Talleyrand, the minister of foreign relations, when I had the honour of being presented to that able and celebrated politician by Mr. B. The hotel of Talleyrand is very superb. We entered the court yard through two lines of about twenty carriages in waiting. Under the portico, were several turks seated, who formed a part of the suite of the turkish embassador, who had just arrived, and was then closetted with Monsieur T— —.

We passed through several noble apartments, preceded by servants, to a magnificent levee room, in which we met most of the foreign embassadors who were then at the consular court.

After waiting some time, the folding doors of the cabinet opened, the turkish embassy came out, making their grand salams, followed by Talleyrand, in his rich costume of embroidered scarlet, his hair full dressed, and a shining sabre by his side.

In his person, he is small and thin, his face is "pale and penetrating." He always looks obliquely, his small quick eyes and features, very legibly express mildness, wit, and subtilty. His right leg appears contracted. His address is insinuating. As the spirit of aggrandizement, which is said to have actuated the public and private conduct of Monsieur T— — has been so much talked of, it may, perhaps, excite some surprise, when it is mentioned that several persons who know him well, some of whom esteem him, and with some of whom he is not a favourite, declare, notwithstanding the anecdotes related of X Y, and Monsieur Beaucoup d'Argent, in the american prints, that they consider him to be a man, whose mind is raised above the influence of corruption. Monsieur T— — may be classed amongst the rarest curiosities in the revolutionary cabinet. Allied by an illustrious ancestry to the Bourbons, and a royalist from his birth, he was, with unusual celerity, invested with the episcopal robe and crosier[11]. During the temporary triumph of the abstract rights of man, over the practicable rights of reason, he moved with the boisterous cavalcade, with more caution than enthusiasm. Upon the celebrated national recognition of the sovereignty of man's *will*, in the Champs de Mars, the politic minister, adorned in snowy robes, and tricolor ribands, presided at the altar of the republic as its high priest, and bestowed his patriarchal benedictions upon the standard of France, and the banners of her departments.

Some time afterwards, in the shape of a secret unaccredited negotiator, he was discovered in the metropolis of England, and immediately transferred, upon the spread wings of the alien bill, to his own shores. Since that period, after having dissociated and neutralized the most formidable foes of his country, by the subtle stratagems of his consummate diplomacy, we beheld him as the successor of la Croix, armed with the powers, and clothed in the gaudy costume of the minister of foreign relations. In the *polished Babel* of the antichamber of this extraordinary man, I have beheld the starred and glittering representatives of the most distinguished princes of the earth waiting for hours, with exemplary resignation, contemplating themselves, in all their positions, in his reduplicating mirrors, or examining the splendour and exquisite ingenuity of his time pieces, until the silver sound of his little bell announced, that the invoked and lagging moment of ministerial leisure was arrived.

It is certain that few people possess the valuable qualities of imperturbable calmness and self possession, more than Monsieur T——. Balanced by these amiable and valuable qualities, he has been enabled to ride the political whirlwind, and in the diplomatic cabinet, to collect some advantage from the prejudices or passions of all who approached him. The caution and cunning of T—— have succeeded, where the sword and impetuous spirit of Bonaparte would have been unavailing. The splendour of his apartments, and of many of the personages present, displayed a very courtlike appearance, and inclined a stranger, like myself, to think, that nothing of the old government was missing, but the expatriated family of France.

NOTES:

[9] The cause which induced Garrick to visit this unhappy person was, it is said, to render the representation of his King Lear more perfect.

[10] Smithfield.

[11] Monsieur Talleyrand is ex-bishop of Autun.

CHAPTER XIX.

The College of the Deaf and Dumb. — Abbé Sicard. — Bagatelle. — Police. — Grand National Library. — Bonaparte's Review. — Tambour Major of the Consular Regiment. — Restoration of Artillery Colours.

I had long anticipated the delight which I expected to derive from the interesting public lecture of the abbé Sicard, and the examination of his pupils. This amiable and enlightened man presides over an institution which endears his name to humanity, and confers unfading honour upon the nation which cherishes it by its protection and munificence. My reader will immediately conclude that I allude to the College of the Deaf and Dumb. By the genius and perseverance of the late abbé Charles Michael de l'Epée, and his present amiable successor, a race of fellow beings, denied by a privation of hearing, of the powers of utterance, insulated in the midst of multitudes bearing their own image, and cut off from the participation, within sight, of all the endearing intercourses of social life, are restored, as it were, to the blessings of complete existence. The glorious labours of these philanthropists, in no very distant ages, would have conferred upon them, the reputation and honours of beings invested with superhuman influence. By making those faculties which are bestowed, auxiliary to those which are denied, the deaf are taught to hear, and the dumb to speak. A silent representative language, in which the eye officiates for the ear, and communicates the charms of science, and the delights of common intercourse to the mind, with the velocity, facility, and certainty of sound, has been presented to these imperfect children of nature. The plan of the abbé, I believe, is before the world. It cannot be expected, in a fugitive sketch like the present, to attempt an elaborate detail of it. Some little idea of its rudiments may, perhaps, be imparted, by a plain description of what passed on the examination day, when I had the happiness of being present.

On the morning of the exhibition, the streets leading to the College were lined with carriages, for humanity has here made a convert of fashion, and directed her wavering mind to objects from which she

151

cannot retire, without ample and consoling gratification. Upon the lawn, in front of the College, were groups of the pupils, enjoying those sports and exercises which are followed by other children, to whom Providence has been more bountiful. Some of their recreations required calculation, and I observed that their intercourse with each other appeared to be easy, swift, and intelligible. They made some convulsive movements with their mouths, in the course of their communication, which, at first, had rather an unpleasant effect. In the cloister I addressed myself to a genteel looking youth, who did not appear to belong to the College, and requested him to shew me the way to the theatre, in which the lecture was to be delivered. I found he took no notice of me. One of the assistants of the abbé, who was standing near me, informed me, he was deaf and dumb, and made two or three signs, too swift for me to discriminate; the silent youth bowed, took me by the hand, led me into the theatre, and, with the greatest politeness, procured me an excellent seat. The room was very crowded, and in the course of a quarter of an hour after I had entered, every avenue leading to it was completely filled with genteel company. The benches of the auditors of the lecture, displayed great beauty and fashion, a stage, or tribune, appeared in front, behind was a large inclined slate, in a frame, about eight feet high, by six long. On each side of the stage the scholars were placed, and behind the spectators was a fine bust of the founder of the institution, the admirable de l'Epée.

The abbé Sicard mounted the tribune, and delivered his lecture with very pleasing address, in the course of which he frequently excited great applause. The subject of it was an analysis of the language of the deaf and dumb, interspersed with several curious experiments upon, and anecdotes of his pupils. The examination of the scholars next followed. The communication which has been opened to them in this singular manner, is by the *philosophy of grammar*.

The denotation of the tenses was effected by appropriate signs. The hand thrown over the shoulder, expressed the past, when extended, like the attitude of inviting, it denoted the future, and the finger inverted upon the breast, indicated the present tense. A single sign communicated a word, and frequently a sentence. A singular instance of the first occurred. A gentleman amongst the spectators, who appeared to be acquainted with the art of the abbé, was requested to make a sign, to the pupil then under examination, the moment it was made, the scholar chalked upon the slate, in a fine swift flowing hand, "une homme." The pupil erred; the gentleman renewed the sign; when he immediately wrote, "une personne," to the astonishment of every person present. This circumstance is a strong instance of the powers of discrimination, of which this curious communication is susceptible.

Some of the spectators requested the abbé to describe, by signs, several sentences which they repeated from memory, or read from authors, which were immediately understood by the pupils, and penciled upon the slate.

The lecture and examination lasted about three hours. Upon the close of this interesting exhibition, a silent sympathy reigned throughout the spectators. Every face beamed with satisfaction. A tear was seen trembling in the eyes of many present. After a momentary pause, the hall rang with acclamations. Elegant women pressed forward in the crowd, to present some little token of their delighted feelings to the children protected by this institution. It was a spectacle, in which genius was observed assisting humanity, and nature in a suffusion of gratitude, weeping over the hallowed and propitious endeavours of the good, the generous, and the enlightened. Well might the elegant and eloquent Kotzebue select from such a spot, a subject for his pathetic pen, and give to the british Roscius of the present day[12], the power of enriching its drama, by a fresh display of his unrivalled abilities. The exhibition of the Deaf and Dumb will never be eradicated from my mind. The tears which were shed on that day, seemed almost sufficient to wipe away the recollection of those times, in which misery experienced no mitigation; when every one trembling for himself, had no unabsorbed sensation of consoling pity to bestow upon the unfortunate. Those times are gone—May their absence be eternal! This institution is made serviceable to the state. A pupil of the College is one of the chief clerks of the national lottery office, in which he distinguishes himself by his talents, his calculation, and upright deportment.

Whilst the subject is before me, I beg leave to mention a curious circumstance which was related by a very ingenious and honourable man, in a party where I happened to be present, to prove the truth and agreement of nature, in her association of ideas. A blind man was asked by him, to what sound he resembled the sensation produced by touching a piece of red cloth, he immediately replied, to the sound of a trumpet. A pupil of the College of the Deaf and Dumb, who could faintly hear a loud noise, if applied close to his ear, was asked, to what colour he could compare the sound of a trumpet, he said, it always excited in his mind, the remembrance of scarlet cloth[13]. Two pupils, male and female, of the same College, who had been placed near cannon, when discharged, without being susceptible of the sound, were one day taken by their humane tutor, into a room where the harmonica was playing; a musical instrument, which is said to have a powerful influence over the nerves. He asked them by signs, if they felt any sensation. They replied in the negative. He then placed the hand of the girl upon the instrument, whilst it was playing, and repeated the question, she answered, that she felt a new pleasure enter the ends of her fingers, pass up her arms, and penetrate her heart.

The same experiment was tried upon her companion, who seemed to be sensible of similar sensations of delight, but less acutely felt.

The emotions of sympathy are, perhaps, more forcibly excited by music than by any other cause. An illustrious example of its effect is introduced into Boerhaave's academical lectures on the diseases of the nerves, published by Van Eems. Theodosius the Great, by levying an excessive tribute, inflamed the minds of the people of Antioch against him, who prostrated his statues, and slew his ambassadors.

Upon coolly reflecting on what they had done, and remembering the stern and ruthless nature of their sovereign, they sent deputies to implore his clemency and forgiveness. The tyrant received them, without making any reply. His chief minister lamenting the condition of these unhappy people, resolved upon an expedient to move the soul of his offended prince to mercy. He accordingly instructed the youths whose office it was to entertain the emperor with music during dinner, to perform an affecting and pathetic piece of music, composed for the purpose. The plaintive sounds soon began to operate. The emperor, unconscious of the cause, bedewed his cup with tears, and when the singers artfully proceeded to describe the sufferings of the people of Antioch, their imperial master could no longer contain himself, but, moved by their pathos, although unaccustomed to forgive, revoked his vengeance, and restored the terrified offenders to his royal favour.

Madame E——, who is considered the first dilettante mistress of music in Paris, related to me, an experiment which she once tried upon a young woman who was totally deaf and dumb. Madame E—— fastened a silk thread about her mouth, and rested the other end upon her piano forte, upon which she played a pathetic air. Her visitor soon appeared much affected, and at length burst into tears. When she recovered, she wrote down upon a piece of paper, that she had experienced a delight, which she could not express, and that it had forced her to weep.

I must reluctantly retire from this pleasing subject, by wishing that the abbé may long enjoy a series of blissful years, and that his noble endeavours, "manifesting the enlightened times in which we live," may meet with that philanthropic success, which, to *his* generous mind, will be its most desired reward *here*; assured, as he is, of being crowned with those unfading remunerations which are promised to the good *hereafter*.

I one day dined at Bagatelle, which is about four miles from Paris, in the Bois du Bologne, the parisian Hyde Park, in which the fashionable equestrian, upon his norman hunter,

— — — — — — — — —"with heel insidiously aside,
Provokes the canter which he seems to chide."

Bagatelle in the Bois de Boulogne.

The duellist also, in the covert windings of this vast wood, seeks reparation for the trifling wrong, and bleeds himself, or slaughters his antagonist. Bagatelle was formerly the elegant little palace of the count d'Artois. The gardens and grounds belonging to it, are beautifully disposed. What a contrast to the gloomy shades of Holyrood House, in which the royal fugitive, and his wretched followers, have found an asylum!

The building and gardens are in the taste of the Petit Trianon, but inferior to it. As usual, it is the residence of cooks, and scullions, tenants of the government, who treat their visitors with good dinners, and excellent wine, and take good care to make them pay handsomely for their faultless fare.

Returning to my hotel rather late at night, I passed through the Champs Elisees, which, at this hour, seemed to be in all its glory. Every "alley green," was filled with whispering lovers. On all sides the sounds of festivity, of music, and dancing, regaled the ear. The weather was very sultry, and being a little fatigued with rather a long walk, I entered through a trellis palisade into a capacious pavilion, where I refreshed myself with lemonade.

Here I found a large bourgeois party enjoying themselves, after the labours of the day, with the waltz, and their favourite beverage, lemonade. A stranger is always surprised at beholding the grace, and activity, which even the lowest orders of people in France, display in dancing. Whiskered corporals, in thick dirty boots, and young tradesmen, in long great coats, led off their respective femmes de chambre and grisettes, with an elegance, which is not to be surpassed in the jewelled birth night ball room. Nothing could exceed the sprightly carelessness, and gay indifference which reigned throughout. The music in this place, as in every other of a similar description, was excellent.

The french police, notwithstanding the invidious rumours which have been circulated to its prejudice, is the constant subject of admiration with every candid foreigner, who is enabled under the shelter of its protection, to perambulate in safety every part of Paris, and its suburbs, although badly lighted, at that hour of the night, which in England, seldom fails to expose the unwary wanderer to the pistol of the prowling ruffian. An enlightened friend of mine, very shrewdly observed, that the english police seems to direct its powers, and consideration more to the apprehension of the robber, than to the prevention of the robbery. In no country is the *art* of thief catching carried higher, than in England. In France, the police is in the highest state of respectability, and unites force to vigilance. The depredator who is fortunate enough to escape the former, is seldom able to elude the latter.

The grand National Library of Paris, is highly deserving of a visit, and is considered to be the first of its kind in Europe. In one of the rooms is a museum of antiques. The whole is about to be removed to the old palace. In one of the wings of this noble collection, are the two celebrated great globes, which rest upon the ground, and rise through the flooring of the first story, where there is a railing round them. These globes I should suppose to be about eighteen feet high.

From the Grand National Library, I went with a party to the military review of all the regiments in Paris, and its suburbs by the first consul, in the Place de Carousel, within the gates, and railing which he has raised for this purpose. We were introduced into the apartments of general Duroc, the governor of the palace, which were upon the ground floor of the Thuilleries, and which afforded us an uninterrupted view of the whole of this superb military spectacle. A little before twelve o'clock, all the regiments of horse and foot, amounting to about 7000 men, had formed the line, when the consular regiment entered, preceded by their fine band, and the tambour major, who was dressed in great magnificence. This man is remarked in Paris for his symmetry and manly beauty. The cream-coloured charger of Bonaparte, upon which, "labouring for destiny, he has often made dreadful way in the field of battle," next passed us, led by grooms in splendid liveries of green and gold, to the grand entrance. As the clock struck twelve, the first consul, surrounded by a chosen body of the consular guard, appeared and mounted. He immediately rode off in full speed, to the gate nearest to the gallery of the Louvre, followed by his favourite generals, superbly attired, mounted upon chargers very richly caparisoned. My eye, aided by a good opera-glass, was fixed upon the first consul. I beheld before me a man whose renown is sounded through the remotest regions of the earth, and whose exploits have been united by the worshippers of favoured heroism to those of the conqueror of Darius. His features are small and meagre. His countenance is melancholy, cold and desperate. His nose is aquiline. His eyes are dark, fiery, and full of genius. His hair, which he wears cropped and without powder, is black. His figure is small, but very muscular. He wore a blue coat, with broad white facings and golden epaulets (the uniform of his regiment) a small cocked hat, in which was a little national cockade. In his hand he carried a small riding whip. His boots were made in the fashion of english riding boots, which I have before condemned on account of their being destitute of military appearance. The reason why they are preferred by the french officers is on account of the top leather not soiling the knees of the pantaloons when in the act of putting one leg over the other. Bonaparte rode through the lines. His beautiful charger seemed conscious of the glory of his rider, and bore him through the ranks with a commanding and majestic pace. The colours of one of the regiments was stationed close under the window, where I had the good fortune of being placed. Here the hero stopped, and saluted them. At this time I was close to him, and had the pleasure of completely gratifying that curiosity of beholding the persons of distinguished men, which is so natural to all of us.

A few minutes after Bonaparte had passed, I saw a procession, the history of which I did not understand at the time, but which fully explained its general purport. About two years since, one of the regiments of artillery revolted in battle. Bonaparte in anger deprived them of their colours, and suspended them, covered with crape, amongst the captive banners of the enemy, in the Hall of Victory. The regiment, affected by the disgrace, were determined to recover the lost esteem of their general and their country, or perish to the last man. When any desperate enterprise was to be performed, they volunteered their services, and by this magnanimous compunction covered their shame with laurels, and became the boast and pride of the republican legions. This day was fixed upon for the restoration of their ensigns. They were marched up under a guard of honour, and presented to the first consul, who took the black drapery from their staves, tore it in pieces, threw it on the ground, and drove his charger indignantly over it. The regenerated banners were then restored to the regiment, with a short and suitable address. I faintly heard this laconic speech, but not distinctly enough to offer any criticism upon the eloquence of the speaker. This exhibition had its intended effect, and displayed the genius of this extraordinary man, who, with unerring acuteness, knows so well to give to every public occurrence that dramatic hue and interest which are so gratifying to the minds of the people over whom he presides. After this ceremony, the several regiments, preceded by their bands of music, marched before him in open order, and dropped their colours as they passed. The flying artillery and cavalry left the parade in full gallop, and made a terrific noise upon the pavement. Each field-piece was drawn by six horses, upon a carriage with large wheels. Here the review closed.

"Farewell, the neighing steed, and the shrill trump,
The spirit-stirring drum, the ear-piercing fife,
The royal banner, and all quality,
Pride, pomp and circumstance of glorious war."

Bonaparte returned to the palace, where he held a splendid levee, at which the new turkish embassy was introduced.

In the evening I saw Bonaparte and his lady at the opera, where he was received with respect, but without any clamorous acclamation.

Madame Bonaparte appears to be older than the first consul. She is an elegant woman, and is said to conduct herself in her high station with becoming dignity and prudence.

NOTES:

[12] Mr. Kemble brought out the pathetic play of Deaf and Dumb, in which he sustains the character of the abbé de l'Epée with admirable effect.

[13] The first experiment is well known. It is also noticed in Locke upon the Human Understanding.

CHAPTER XX.

Abbè Sieyes. — Consular Procession to the Council Chamber. — 10th of August, 1792. — Celerity of Mons. Fouche's Information. — The two Lovers. — Cabinet of Mons. le Grand — Self-prescribing Physician. — Bust of Robespierre. — His Lodgings. — Corn Hall. — Museum of French Monuments. — Revolutionary Agent. — Lovers of married Women.

A neat remark was made upon the abbè Sieyes, to whose prolific mind the revolution and all its changes have been imputed. This extraordinary man has a noble house in the Champs Elisées, and is said to have the best cook in Paris. As a party in which I was, were passing his hotel, a near relation of the abbè, who happened to be with us, commented upon the great services which the cloistered fabricator of constitutions had afforded to France, and adverted to his house and establishment as an unsuitable reward for his labours. A gentleman, who was intimate with the abbè, but was no great admirer of his morals, said, "I think, my dear madam, the abbè ought to be very well satisfied with his destiny; and I would advise him to live as long as he can in the Champs Elisées; for when he shall happen to experience that mysterious transition to which we are all hastening, I think the chances will be against his finding good accommodations in any other Elysium."

As I was passing one morning through the hall of the Thuilleries, the great door of the council chamber was opened, and the second and third consuls, preceded and followed by their suite in full costume, *marched* with great pomp to business, to the roll of a drum. This singular procession from one part of the house to the other, had a ridiculous effect, and naturally reminded me of the fustian pageantry which, upon the stage, attends the entries and exits of the kings and queens of the drama.

I have often been surprised to find that the injuries which the cornice of the entrance, and the capitals of the columns in the hall of the Thuilleries, have sustained from the ball of cannon, during the horrible massacre of the 10th of August, 1792, have never been repaired. Every vestige of that day of dismay and slaughter ought for ever to be effaced; instead of which, some labour has been exercised to perpetuate its remembrance. Under the largest chasms which have been made by the shot is painted, in strong characters, that gloomy date.

In the evening of that day of devastation, from which France may date all her sufferings, a friend of mine went into the court-yard of the Thuilleries, where the review is now held, for the purpose of endeavouring to recognise, amongst the dead, any of his acquaintances. In the course of this shocking search, he declared to me, that he counted no less than eight hundred bodies of Swiss and French, who had perished in that frightful contest between an infatuated people and an irresolute sovereign. I will not dilate upon this painful subject, but dismiss it in the words of the holy and resigned descendant of Nahor, "Let that day be darkness; let not God regard it from above, neither let the light shine upon it; let darkness and the shadow of death stain it; let a cloud dwell upon it; let the blackness of the day terrify it."

I have before had occasion to notice the promptitude and activity of the french police, under the penetrating eye of Mons. Fouche. No one can escape the vigilance of this man and his emissaries. An emigrant of respectability assured me, that when he and a friend of his waited upon him for their passports to enable them to quit Paris for the South of France, he surprised them by relating to them the names of the towns, the streets, and of the people with whom they had lodged, at various times, during their emigration in England.

Whilst I was at Paris, an affair happened very near the hotel in which I lodged, which in its sequel displayed that high spirit and sensibility which appear to form the presiding features in the french character, to which may be attributed all the excesses which have stained, and all the glory which has embellished it. A lady of fortune, and her only daughter, an elegant and lovely young woman, resided in the Fauxbourg St. Germain. A young man of merit and accomplishments, but unaided by the powerful pretensions of suitable fortune, cherished a passion for the young lady, to whom he had frequent access, on account of his being distantly related to her. His affection was requited with return; and before the parent suspected the attachment, the lovers were solemnly engaged. The indications of pure love are generally too unguarded to escape the keen, observing eye of a cold, mercenary mother. She charged her daughter with her fondness, and forbade her distracted lover the house. To close up every avenue of hope, she withdrew with her wretched child into Italy, where they remained for two years; at the expiration of which, the mother had arranged for her daughter a match more congenial to her own pride and avarice, with an elderly gentleman, who had considerable fortune and property in the vicinity of Bourdeaux. Every necessary preparation was made for this cruel union, which it was determined should be celebrated in Paris, to which city they returned for that purpose. Two days before the marriage was intended to take place, the young lover, wrought up to frenzy by the intelligence of the approaching nuptials, contrived, by bribing the porter whilst the mother was at the opera with her intended son-in-law, to reach the room of the beloved being from whom he was about to be separated for ever. Emaciated by grief, she presented the mere spectre of what she was when he last left her. As soon as he entered the room, he fell senseless at her feet, from which state he was roused by the loud fits of her frightful maniac laughter. She stared upon him, like one bewildered. He clasped her with one hand, and with the other drew from his pocket a vial containing double distilled laurel water: he pressed it to her lips, until she had swallowed half of its contents; the remainder he drank himself.—The drug of death soon began to operate.—Clasped in each other's arms, pale and expiring, they reviewed their hard fate, and, in faint and lessening sentences, implored of the great God of mercy, that he would pardon them for what they had done, and that he would receive their spirits into his regions of eternal repose; that he would be pleased, in his divine goodness, to forgive the misjudging severity which had driven them to despair, and would support the unconscious author of it, under the heavy afflictions which their disastrous deaths would occasion. They had scarcely finished their prayer, when they heard footsteps approaching the room. Madame R——, who had been indisposed at the opera, returned home before its conclusion, with the intended bridegroom.

The young man awoke, as it were, from his deadly drowsiness, and, exerting his last strength, pulled from his breast a dagger, stabbed the expiring being, upon whom he doated, to the heart; and, falling upon her body, gave himself several mortal wounds. The door opened; the frantic mother appeared. All the house was in an instant alarmed; and the fatal explanation which furnished the materials of this short and sad recital, was taken from the lips of the dying lover, who had scarcely finished it before he breathed his last. Two days afterwards, the story was hawked about the streets.

From this painful narrative, in which the French impetuosity is strongly depicted, I must turn to mention my visit to Mons. le G——, who lives in the Rue Florentine, and is considered to be one of the first architects in France; in which are many monuments of his taste and elegance. It is a curious circumstance that all artists exercise their talents more successfully for their patrons than for themselves. Whether it is the hope of a more substantial reward than that of mere self-complacency, which usually excites the mind to its happiest exertions, I will not pretend to determine; but the point seems to be in some degree settled by the conduct of a celebrated Bath physician, of whom it is related, that, happening once to suffer under a malady from which as his skill had frequently relieved others, he determined to prescribe for himself. The recipe at first had not the desired effect. The doctor was surprised. At last he recollected that he had not feed himself. Upon making this discovery, he drew the strings of his purse, and with his left hand placed a guinea in his right, and then prescribed. The story concludes by informing its readers, that the prescription succeeded, and the doctor recovered.—In adorning the front of his own hôtel, Mons. le G——, in my very humble opinion, has not exhibited his accustomed powers. In a small confined court-yard he has attempted to give to a private dwelling the appearance of one of those vast temples of which he became enamoured when at Athens. The roof is supported by two massy fluted pilastres, which in size are calculated to bear the burthen of some prodigious dome. The muscular powers of Hercules seem to be here exercised in raising a grasshopper from the ground. The genius of Mons. le G——, unlike the world's charity, does not begin at home, but seems more disposed to display its most successful energies abroad. His roof, however, contains such a monument of his goodness and generosity, that I must not pass it over. This distinguished architect is one of those unfortunate beings who have been decreed to taste the bitterness, very soon after the sweets of matrimony. Upon discovering the infidelity of his lady, who is very pretty and prepossessing, the distracted husband immediately sought a divorce from the laws of his country. This affair happened a very short time before the revolution afforded unusual acceleration and facilities to the wishes of parties, who, under similar circumstances, wished to get rid of each other as soon as possible. The then "law's delay" afforded some cause of vexation to Mons. le G— —, who was deeply injured. Before his suit had passed through its last forms, the father of his wife, who at the time of their marriage lived in great affluence, became a bankrupt. In the vortex of his failure, all the means of supporting his family were swallowed up. The generous le G— —, disdaining to expose to want and ignominy the woman who had once been dear to him, would proceed no further. She is still his wife; she bears his name, is maintained by him, and in a separate suite of apartments lives under the same roof with him. But Mons. and Madame le G— — have had no intercourse whatever with each other for eleven years. If in the gallery or in the hall they meet by accident, they pass without the interchange of a word. This painful and difficult arrangement has now lost a considerable portion of its misery, by having become familiar to the unfortunate couple.

In the valuable and curious cabinet of Mons. le G— —, I found out, behind several other casts, a bust of Robespierre, which was taken of him, a short period before he fell. A tyrant, whose offences look white, contrasted with the deep delinquency of the oppressor of France, is said to be indebted more to his character, than to nature, for the representation of that deformity of person which appears in Shakspeare's portrait of him, when he puts this soliloquy in his lips: —

"I that am curtail'd of this fair proportion,
Cheated of feature, by dissembling Nature,
Deform'd, unfinish'd, sent before my time,
Into the breathing world, scarce half made up;

And that so lamely and unfashionably,
That dogs bark at me, as I halt by them."

History, enraged at the review of the insatiable crimes of Robespierre, has already bestowed upon him a fanciful physiognomy, which she has composed of features which rather correspond with the ferocity of his soul, than with his real countenance. From the appearance of this bust, which is an authentic resemblance of him, his face must have been rather handsome. His features were small, and his countenance must have strongly expressed animation, penetration and subtlety. This bust is a real curiosity. It is very likely that not another is now to be found, Mons. le G—— is permitted to preserve it, without reproach on account of his art. I can safely say, he does not retain it from any emotions of veneration for the original. It is worthy of being placed between the heads of Caligula and Nero. Very near the residence of Mons. le G—— is the house in which Robespierre lodged. It is at the end of the Rue Florentine, in the Rue St. Honore, at a wax chandler's. This man is too much celebrated, not to render every thing which relates to him curious. The front windows of his former lodgings look towards the Place de la Concorde, on the right of which his prime minister, the permanent guillotine, was quartered. Robespierre, who, like the revolting angel, before the world's formation, appears to have preferred the sceptre of Hell and chaos, to the allegiance of order and social happiness, will descend to posterity with no common attributes of distinction and preeminence. His mind was fully suited to its labours, which, in their wide sphere of mischief, required more genius to direct them than was bestowed upon the worst of the tyrants of Rome, and a spirit of evil which, with its "broad circumference" of guilt, was calculated to darken the disk of their less expanded enormity.

From Robespierre's lodgings, curiosity led me to visit the building in which the jacobin club held their Pandemonium. It is a noble edifice, and once belonged to the Order of Jacobins. Near this church stands the beautiful fabric of the Corn Hall of Paris, designed by Monsieur le Grand. The dome of the bank of England is in the same style, but inferior, in point of lightness and elegance. That of the Corn Hall resembles a vast concavity of glass. In this noble building the millers deposit their corn for sale. Its deep and lofty arches and area, were nearly filled with sacks, containing that grain which is precious to all nations, but to none more than the french; to a frenchman, bread is most emphatically the staff of life. He consumes more of it at one meal than an englishman does at four. In France, the little comparative quantity of bread which the english consume, is considered to form a part of their national character. Before I left Paris, I was requested to visit a very curious and interesting exhibition, the Museum of French Monuments; for the reception of which, the ancient convent of the monks of the Order of les Petits Augustines, is appropriated. This national institution is intended to exhibit the progress of monumental taste in France, for several centuries past, the specimens of which have chiefly been collected from St. Denis, which formerly was the burial place of the monarchs of France, and from other churches.

Museum of French Monuments.

It will be remembered by the reader, that in the year 1793, Henriot, a vulgar and furious republican, proposed setting off for the former church, at the head of the sans culottes, to destroy all these curious and valuable relics, "to strike," as he said, "the tyrants in their tombs," but was prevented by some other republicans of influence, who had not parted with their veneration for works of taste, from this impious and impotent outrage.

In the first hall, which is very large, and impresses a similar awe to that which is generally felt upon entering a cathedral, are the tombs of the twelfth century. Amongst them I chiefly distinguished that of Henry II, upon which are three beautiful mourning figures, supporting a cup, containing his heart.

In the second hall, are the monuments of the thirteenth century, most of them are very fine; that of Lewis the XIIth and his queen, is well worthy of notice. I did not find much to gratify me in the hall of the fourteenth century. In that of the fifteenth century are several noble tombs, and beautiful windows of stained glass. In the hall of the sixteenth century is a fine statue of Henry the IVth, by Franchville, which is considered to be an admirable likeness of that wonderful man. In the hall of the seventeenth century, is a noble figure, representing religion, by Girardon.

In the cloisters are several curious statues, stained glass windows, and tesselated pavement. There is here also a good bust of Alexis Peron, with this singular epitaph,

Ci git qui ne fut rien,
Pas même académicien.

In the square garden within the cloisters, are several ancient urns, and tombs. Amongst them is the vase which contains the ashes, if any remain, of Abelard and Heloise, which has been removed from the Paraclete to the Museum. It is covered with the graceful shade of an Acacia tree, which seems to wave proudly over its celebrated deposit. Upon approaching this treasurable antique, all those feelings rushed in upon me, which the beautiful, and affecting narrative of those disastrous lovers, by Pope, has often excited in me. The melancholy Heloise seemed to breathe from her tomb here,

"If ever chance two wandering lovers brings,
O'er the pale marble shall they join their heads,
And drink the falling tear each other sheds:
Then sadly say, with mutual pity mov'd,
Oh! may we never love, as these have lov'd."

National guards are stationed in every apartment of the Museum, and present rather an unaccording appearance, amidst the peaceful solemnity of the surrounding objects. This exhibition is not yet completed, but, in its present condition, is very interesting. Some hints, not altogether useless, may be collected from it. In England, our churches are charnel houses. The pews of the congregation are raised upon foundations of putrefaction. For six days and nights the temple of devotion is filled with the pestilent vapours of the dead, and on the seventh they are absorbed by the living. Surely it is high time to subdue prejudices, which endanger health without promoting piety. The scotch never bury in their churches, and their burial places are upon the confines of their towns. The eye of adoration is filled with a pensive pleasure, in observing itself surrounded with the endeavours of taste and ingenuity, to lift the remembrance of the great and good beyond the grave, in that very spot where the frailty of our nature is so often inculcated.

Such a display, in such a place, is rational, suitable, and admonitory. The silent tomb becomes auxiliary to the eloquence of the pulpit. But the custom which converts the place of worship into a catacomb, can afford but a mistaken consolation to posthumous pride, and must, in some degree, contaminate the atmosphere which is contained within its walls. One evening as I was passing through the Boulevard Italien, in company with a gentleman from Toulon, we met a tall, dark, hollow eyed, ferocious looking man, of whom he related the following story.

Immediately after the evacuation of Toulon by the english, all the principal toulonese citizens were ordered to repair to the market place; where they were surrounded by a great military force.

This man who, for his offences, had been committed to prison, was liberated by the french agents, in consequence of his undertaking to select those of the inhabitants who had in any manner favoured the capitulation of the town, or who had shown any hospitality to the english, whilst they were in possession of it. The miscreant passed before the citizens, who were drawn out in lines, amounting to near three thousand. Amongst whom he pointed out about one thousand four hundred persons to the fury of the government; without any other evidence, or further examination, they were all immediately adjudged to be shot. For this purpose a suitable number of soldiers were drawn out. The unhappy victims were marched up to their destruction, upon the quay, in sets of three hundred, and butchered.

The carnage was dreadful. In the last of these unfortunate groups, were two gentlemen of great respectability, who received no wound from the fire, but, to preserve themselves, dropped with the rest, and exhibited all the appearances of having participated in the general fate.

This execution took place in the evening: immediately after its close, the soldiers, fatigued, and sick with cold-blooded slaughter, marched back to their quarters, without examining whether every person upon whom they had fired, had fallen a victim to the murderous bullet. Soon after the soldiers had retired, the women of Toulon, allured by plunder, proceeded to the fatal spot. Mounted upon the bodies of the fallen, they stripped the dead, and dying. The night was stormy. The moon, emerging from dark clouds, occasionally, shed its pale lustre upon this horrible scene. When the plunderers had abandoned their prey, during an interval of deep darkness, in the dead of the night, when all was silent, unconscious of each other's intentions, the two citizens who had escaped the general carnage, disencumbered themselves from the dead, under whom they were buried; chilled and naked, in an agony of mind not to be described, they, at the same moment, attempted to escape. In their agitation, they rushed against each other. Expressions of terror and surprise, dropped from each of them. "Oh! God! it is my father!" said one, "my son, my son, my son," exclaimed the other, clasping him in his arms. They were father and son, who had thus miraculously escaped, and met in this extraordinary manner.

The person from whom I received this account, informed me, that he knew these gentlemen very well, and that they had been resettled in Toulon about two years.

The wretch who had thus directed the ruthless vengeance of a revolutionary banditti, against the breasts of his fellow citizens, was, at this time, in Paris, soliciting, from the present government, from a total misconception of its nature, those remunerations which had been promised, but never realized by his barbarous employers.

I need scarcely add, that although he had been in the capital several months, he had not been able to gain access to the minister's secretary.

The time of terror was over—the murderer's occupation was gone—the guillotine, with unsatiated hunger, after having gorged the food which was thrown to it, had devoured its feeder.

I must leave it to the ingenuity of my reader, to connect the observation with which I shall close this chapter, with the preceding story, for I am only enabled to do so, by observing, that an impressive instance of the subject of it, occurred immediately after my mind had been harrowed up, by the narrative which I have just related. The married women of France feel no compunctious visitings of conscience, in cherishing about them a circle of lovers, amongst whom their husbands are *merely* more favoured than the rest. I hope I shall not be considered as an apologist, for an indulgence which, in France, excites no jealousy in *one*, and no surprise amongst the many, when I declare, that I confidently believe, in most instances, it commences, and guiltlessly terminates in the love of admiration. I know, and visited in Paris, a most lovely and accomplished young woman, who had been married about two years. She admitted the visits of men, whom she knew were passionately fond of her. Sometimes she received them in the presence, and sometimes in the absence of her husband, as accident, not arrangement, directed. They approached her with all the agitation and tenderness of the most ardent lovers. Amongst the number, was a certain celebrated orator. This man was her abject slave. A glance from her expressive eye raised him to the summit of bliss, or rendered his night sleepless. The complacent husband of Madame G—— regarded these men as his most beloved friends, because they enlarged the happiness of his wife; and, strange as it may appear, I believe that he had as little cause to complain as Othello, and therefore never permitted his repose to be disturbed by those suspicions which preyed upon the vitals of the hapless moor. The french Benedict might truly exclaim,

> "—————————'Tis not to make me jealous,
> To say my wife is fair, feeds well, loves company,
> Is free of speech, sings, plays, and dances well;
> Where virtue is, these are more virtuous;
> Nor from my own weak merits will I draw
> The smallest fear, or doubt of her revolt."

CHAPTER XXI.

Picturesque and Mechanical Theatre. —Filtrating and purifying Vases. —
English Jacobins. —A Farewell. —Messagerie. —Mal Maison. —Forest of
Evreux. —Lower Normandy. —Caen. —Hon. T. Erskine. —A Ball. —The
Keeper of the Sachristy of Notre Dame. —The two blind Beggars. —
Ennui. —St. Lo. —Cherbourg. —England.

I visited, one evening, a very beautiful exhibition, which I think worthy of being noticed; it was the picturesque and mechanical theatre. The company present were select and genteel. The room and stage were upon a small scale; the former was very elegantly fitted up. The spectacle consisted of scenery and appropriate little moving figures. The first scene was a view of a wood in early morning, every object looked blue, fresh, and dewy. The gradations of light, until the approach of meridian day, were admirably represented. Serpents were seen crawling in the grass. A little sportsman entered with his fowling-piece, and imitated all the movements natural to his pursuit; a tiny wild duck rose from a lake, and flew before him. He pointed his gun, changed his situation, pointed it again, and fired. The bird dropped; he threw it over his shoulders, fastened to his gun, and retired. Waggons, drawn by horses about four inches high, passed along; groups of peasantry followed, exquisitely imitating all the indications of life. Amongst several other scenes was a beautiful view of the bay of Naples, and the great bridge; over which little horses, with their riders, passed in the various paces of walking, trotting and galloping. All the minutiæ of nature were attended to. The ear was beguiled with the patting of the horses' hoofs upon the pavement; and some of the little animals reared, and ran before the others. There were also some charming little sea-pieces, in which the vessels sailed with their heads towards the spectators, and manœuvred in a surprising manner. The whole concluded with a storm and shipwreck. Sailors were seen floating in the water, then sinking in the surge. One of them rose again and reached a rock. Boats put off to his relief, and perished in the attempt. The little figure was seen displaying the greatest agonies. The storm subsided; tiny persons appeared upon the top of a projecting cliff, near a watch tower, and lowered a rope to the little sufferer below, which he caught, and, after ascending to some height by it, overwhelmed with fatigue, lost his hold. After recovering from the fall, he renewed his efforts, and at length reached the top in safety, amidst the acclamations of the spectators, who, moved by this enchanting little illusion, took much interest in the apparent distress of the scene.

Upon quitting the theatre, we found a real storm without. The lightning flamed upon us from every quarter, and was succeeded by loud peals of thunder. Whilst we were contemplating the tempest from the balcony of Madame S— —, a ball of fire fell very near us, and filled the room with a sulphureous stench. A servant soon afterwards entered, almost breathless, to inform his mistress, Madame R— —, who was of the party, that the fire-ball had penetrated her house, which was close adjoining, without having effected any injury. Madame R— — laughed heartily, and observed, "Well, it is very droll that the lightning should make so free with my house when I am not at home." This little sprightly remark dispersed the gloom which had overshadowed most of the ladies present. All the large houses in Paris are well protected against the perilous effect of electric fluid, by conductors, which are very judiciously disposed.

An invention has lately made its appearance in Paris, which is as full of utility as it is of genius. A house has been lately opened for the sale of filtrating and purifying vases, to which the ingenious constructor has given the most elegant etruscan shapes. They are capable of refining the most fetid and corrupt water, by a process which, in its operation, lasts about four minutes. The principle is the same as in nature. The foul water is thrown into the vase, where it passes through various strata of earth, which are compressed in a series of little apartments, which retain its offensive particles, and from which it issues as clear and as sweet as rock water. This discovery will prove of infinite consequence to families who reside in the maritime parts of Holland, and to many inland towns in France, where the water is frequently very bad. I most cordially hope that the inventor will meet with the remuneration which is due to his humane philosophy.

After having experienced a most cordial display of kindnesses and hospitalities, I prepared to return to my own country, "that precious stone set in the silver sea." I had to part with those who, in the short space of one fleeting month, had, by their endearing and flattering attentions, rivetted themselves to my affections, with the force of a long, and frequent, and cherished intercourse, who, in a country where I expected to feel the comfortless sensations of a foreigner, made me forget that I was even a *stranger*. Amongst those who excited a considerable share of my regret upon parting, were the elegant and charming family of the S——s. As I was preparing to take my leave, Madame S—— said, "You must not forget us because a few waves divide our countries."

"If he will lend me his pocket-book," said one of her lovely daughters, "I will try and see if my pencil will not preserve us in his memory, at least for a little time."

I presented it to her, and in a few minutes she made an elegant little sketch, which she called "The affectionate Mother." Amiable young artist! may Time, propitious to the happiness of some generous being, who is worthy of such an associate, hail thee with the blissful appellation! and may the graceful discharge of those refined and affecting duties which flow from connubial love, entitle thee, too much esteemed to be envied, to the name of the modern Cornelia!

Several Englishmen, whilst I was at Paris, met with very vexatious delays in procuring their passports to enable them to leave it, from a mistaken course of application. Instead of applying to M. Fouche, or any other municipal officer, I would recommend them to procure their passport from their own embassador, and send it to the office of Mons. Talleyrand for his endorsement; by which means they will be enabled to quit the republic in two or three days after their application.

Having previously determined to return by the way of Lower Normandy, upon the beauty and luxuriance of which I had heard much eulogy, about half past five o'clock in the morning of the 21st of Prairial, I left my hotel, and proceeded to the Messagerie, from which the diligences, all of which are under the control of the nation, set out. The morning was very beautiful. I was much entertained before I mounted that cumbrous vehicle, which was to roll me a little nearer to my own coast, by viewing the numerous groups of travellers and their friends, who surrounded the different carriages as the horses were tackling to them. In different directions of my eye, I saw about thirty men kissing each other. The women in France never think their prerogatives infringed by this anti-anglo mode of salutation. Some shed tears at parting; but the cheek down which they trickled never lost its colour or vivacity. All were animated; every eye looked bright; there was a gayety in their very grief. "Bon voyage, bon voyage—Dieu vous benisse, Dieu vous benisse," reiterated on all sides from sprightly faces, stretched out of the window frames of the massy machine, as it rattled through the gates of the yard, to the incessant crackings of the postilion's long lash. I soon afterwards found myself seated in the diligence for Cherbourg, in company with two ladies, and three gentlemen, who were all polite and pleasing. In the cabriole, forward, was a french captain in the army, who had been in Tippoo's service at the time of the surrender of Seringapatam. He looked abominably dirty in his travelling habiliments; but that, in France, is now no just indication of inferiority or vulgarity.

We passed by the Place de la Concorde, upon the statues and buildings of which, and the gardens of the Thuilleries, the fresh and early sun shone most beautifully. My merry, but feeling fellow travellers, waving their hands, addressed a short apostrophe to these suburb objects, and exclaimed, "adieu ma tres jolie ville—ah! tres jolie ville adieu."

For near three miles after leaving the barrier, we passed through plantations of roses, which supply the markets of Paris with that beautiful flower, which, transferred thence, adorn the toilets, the vases, and the bosoms of the fair parisians, and form the favourite bouquets of the petite maitres; on each side of the road were cherry trees, in full bearing, which presented a very charming appearance. We soon reached the water works of Marli, which supply the jets d'eau of Versailles. They are upon a vast scale, and appear to be very curious. A little further on we passed Mal Maison, the country, and chief residence of the first consul and his family. It is an ancient house, embosomed in beautiful woods and gardens. At the entrance are large military lodges, for the accommodation of a squadron of the consular cavalry, who mount guard when their general is here.

Malmaison.

At St. Germain's we breakfasted, upon pork cutlets, excellent bread, wine, and cherries, for twenty sols, or ten pence english. At Mante we had an excellent dinner, of several dishes, for thirty sols, or one shilling and three pence english. Soon after we had passed Mante, we left the higher norman road, and entered a country extremely picturesque and rich. We were conducted through the forest of Evreux, by an escort of chasseurs. This vast tract of land is infested by an immense banditti, who live in large excavations in the earth, similar to the subterranean apartments of the celebrated robbers, in whose service Gil Blas was rather reluctantly enrolled, and generally assail the traveller, with a force which would render common resistance perilous, and unavailing. This forest, in the course of the year, furnishes considerable employ for the guillotine of Caen, where the tribunal of justice is seated. The appearance of our guards was terrific enough to appal such valiant souls, as once animated the frames of *prince Hal*, and his merry friend *Ned Poins*. They wore roman helmets, from which descended, to the bottom of their backs, an immense tail, of thick black horsehair, their uniform was light green, and looked rather shabby.

We passed the forest without any molestation, and supped at the town of Evreux, which is very pleasant, where we halted for about four hours. As we were afterwards proceeding, I prepared myself to enjoy a little sleep, and as I reclined for this purpose with my hat over my face, in a corner of the carriage, I overheard one of my fellow travellers observe to the other, "the englishman is sleeping," to which he replied, "no, he is not sleeping, he is only thinking, it is the character of his nation."

The french cannot bear the least appearance of thought; they have a saying, "un homme qui rit ne sera jamais dangereux."

The next morning we breakfasted at Lisieux, an ancient town, in which are the remains of a fine convent, which formerly belonged to the Order of the Capuchins. For four or five miles before we approached the town, the laughing and animated faces of groups of peasantry, all in their jubilee dresses, the old mounted upon asses, and the young walking by the sides of them, hastening to the town, announced to us, that a fair, and merry making was to be held there, on that day. Lisieux was quite in a bustle. About six o'clock in the evening of the same day, we arrived at Caen, the capital of Lower Normandy. My fare to this city from Paris, amounted to thirty livres, including my luggage. I had not completed my dinner at the Hôtel de la Place, before an english servant entered my room, to inform me, that his mistress, Mrs. P— —, who, with her daughters, and another young lady, had the rooms over mine, presented her compliments to me, and requested me to take my coffee with them that evening. I must confess I was at first a little surprised at the message, for the english are not very remarkable for politeness and attention to one another in a foreign country.

Caen.

After I had finished my desert, I made my bow to Mrs. P——, and her family, who proved to be very pleasant, and accomplished people, and were making the tour of France with english servants. They had been in Caen near three weeks, where they had a large acquaintance of the first respectability. This unexpected introduction became additionally agreeable, upon my discovery at the Messagerie, that the diligence for Cherbourg would not proceed, till three days from the time of my arrival. The next morning I rambled with my new friends about the city, which is large, and handsome, and is watered by the river Orne. It is much celebrated for its lace trade; on that day I dined with Mrs. P——, and a french party, and was regaled with an english dinner, cooked, and served up by her own servants. The filth of the french kitchen is too well known, to make it necessary for me to say how delicious such a dinner was. The french admit themselves that their cooks are destitute of cleanliness.

The Convent of the Benedictines, which is converted into the palace of the prefect, is a noble building. The gardens belonging to it are well arranged. The promenade called de la Cour is very charming, from which the city is seen to great advantage. The water of the Orne is rather nauseous, but is not considered unwholesome. The Palais de Justice is a fine modern structure. In its courts of law, I had again an opportunity of hearing the forensic elocution of Normandy. The gestures, and vehemence of the orators here, as at Rouen, appeared to me to be tinctured with the extravagance of frenzy. But perhaps my ears, and eyes have been rendered somewhat too fastidious by having been frequently banqueted with the grace, animation, and commanding eloquence of the unrivalled advocate of the british bar; who, when he retires from the laborious duties of the crowded, and admiring forum, where his acute sagacity has so often unfolded the dark compact involutions of human obliquity, where his wit and fancy have covered with the choicest flowers, the dreary barrenness of technical pleading; will leave behind him that lasting, and honourable respect and remembrance, which faculties so extensively beneficial, must ever excite in the minds of men who have been instructed, delighted, and benefited by their splendid, and prosperous display.

In this city was pointed out to me, the house in which the celebrated Charlotte Corday resided, who, by her poniard, delivered France of the monster, Marat, on Sunday, the 14th of July, 1793. There is some coincidence in the crimes, and fate of Caligula and Marat, both perished by the avengers of their country, whilst in the act of approaching their baths. Posterity will embalm, with its grateful remembrance, the patriotic heroism of this great, and distinguished female, and in her own firm, and eloquent language, will say of her, "that crime begets disgrace, and not the scaffold."

On the evening after my arrival at Caen, I was invited to an elegant ball, which was given by the lady of the paymaster general of the district, in one of the government houses. I had before witnessed the dancing of the higher orders of people in Paris, and from this reason was not surprised in contemplating the exquisite grace which was here displayed. The party consisted of near eighty persons. Amongst them were the judges of the district, and the principal officers quartered in the city, and its neighbourhood, the latter were attired in superb military dresses. Amongst the ladies were several beautiful, well dressed young women, who exhibited their persons to great advantage. The grave, and elderly part of the company played at buillotte, which is at present the favourite french game. In

France to please and to be pleased, seem to be the two presiding principles in all their meetings. An elegant young officer, who had distinguished himself at the battle of Marengo, observing that the musicians appeared to be a little fatigued, by the contribution of their exhilarating services towards the festivity of the evening, supplied their room, whilst they refreshed themselves, and struck up an english country dance on one of the violins. The party attempted to dance it, but to show how arbitrary habit is, in the attempt, all those powers of grace, which they had before so beautifully displayed, retired as if influenced by the magic of some unpropitious spirit. Amongst the party, was a little girl, about nine years old, who was dressed in the highest style of fashion, and looked like a fashionable milliner's doll. This little spoiled child was accustomed to spend an hour at her toilette every morning, and to be tricked out in all the ephemeral decoration of the haut ton. This little coquette already looked out for admiration, and its foolish mother expressed the greatest satisfaction, when any one, out of politeness to her, paid attentions to the pert premature nursling. Our entertainment concluded with a handsome supper, and we parted, highly delighted, at the dawn of day. Nothing could be more flattering, than the attentions which, as an englishman, I received from every one present.

After a few hours repose, I went with a large party to the church of Notre Dame; in which there is a very fine altar piece. The keeper of the sachristy, who was a very arch-looking little fellow, in spite of the solemnity of the place in which we were, made us all smile (even a young lady who was going to be confessed for the first time the next day, lost a considerable proportion of her gravity) by informing us, that during the time of terror he had run off with the Virgin Mary, pointing to the image, and that to prevent the detection of Robespierre's agents, he had concealed her in his bed for three years. Nothing could exceed his joy in having saved her from the hatchet, or the flames, from which impending fate, she was restored to her former situation in this church; and was, when we saw her, by the extravagance of her sprightly, and ardent protector, dressed in a white muslin gown, spotted with silver; a little bouquet of artificial flowers graced her bosom, and her wig was finely curled, and powdered. The figure in her arms, which was intended to represent the infant Jesus, was dressed in a style equally unsuitable; his hair was also curled, and powdered, and a small cocked hat placed upon his head. Our delighted guide, whose eyes sparkled with self-complacency, asked us if we had ever seen a prettier Virgin Mary, or one dressed more handsomely. We were all much amused by the quaintness of this man's conduct, although I am confident he had no intention of exciting unbecoming sensations, for in saving this image, he had exposed his life.

From Notre Dame, we went to the Abbaye aux Hommes, built by William the Conqueror. It is a large lofty plain pile of building. The spires are well proportioned, and very high. The pillars in the choir are, in my humble opinion, too massy. Preparations were here making for the celebration of the great festival called the Feast of God. We presented to one of the priests, who, in the sachristy, was adorning the cradle of our Saviour's image with flowers, some very fine moss roses, which in France are very rare, which he received with great politeness. This festival before the revolution was always superbly celebrated. It was then renewed for the first time since the proscription of religion, during which, all the costly habits of the priests, and rich vessels used in the ceremonies of the church have been stolen, sold, or melted down. Near the altar, which has been shattered by the axe of the revolution, is the vault of the norman conqueror.

Upon our return to our hotel, we saw a considerable crowd assembled near the bridge leading to de la Cour. Upon inquiring into the cause of this assemblage, we found it was owing to a curious rencounter between two blind beggars, who, in total darkness, had been waging an uncertain battle for near six minutes. It appeared that one of them had for several months, enjoyed quiet possession of the bridge, which happened to be a great thoroughfare, and had during that time, by an undisputed display of his calamity, contrived to pick up a comfortable recompense for it; that within a few days preceding this novel fracas, another mendicant, who had equal claims to compassion, allured by the repute of his success, had deserted a less frequented part of the city, and had presented himself at the other corner of the same bridge, where by a more masterly selection of moving phrases, he soon not only divided, but monopolized the eleemosynary revenues of this post of wretchedness. The original possessor naturally grew jealous. Even beggars "can bear no brother near the throne." Inflamed with jealousy, he silently moved towards his rival, by the sound of whose voice, which was then sending forth some of its most affecting, and purse-drawing strains, he was enabled to determine whether his arm was within reach of the head of his competitor, which circumstance, having with due nicety ascertained, he clenched his fist, which in weight, size, and firmness, was not much surpassed by the hard, and ponderous paw of a full-grown tiger, and with all the force of that propulsion, which a formidable set of muscles afforded, he felled his rival to the ground, and not knowing that he was fallen, discharged many other blows, which only served to disturb the tranquillity of the air. The recumbent hero, whose head was framed for enterprises of this nature, soon recovered from the assault, and, after many unavailing efforts in the dark, at length succeeded in opening one of the vessels of the broad nose of his brawny assailant, whose blood, enriched by good living, streamed out most copiously. In this condition we saw these orbless combatants, who were speedily separated from each other. Some of the crowd were endeavouring to form a treaty of pacification between them, whether they succeeded I know not, for we were obliged to leave the bridge of battle, before these important points were arranged, to join a pleasant party at Mons. St. J——'s, an opulent banker at Caen, to whom I had letters of introduction from Mons. R——, the banker of Paris.

After spending the short time, during which I was detained at Caen, very pleasantly, I resumed my seat in the diligence for Cherbourg, in which I found a very agreeable woman, her two daughters, two canary birds, a cat, and her kitten, who were, I found, to be my companions all the way. After we left Caen, the roads became very bad. Our ponderous machine, frequently rolled from one side to the other, and with many alarming creakings, threatened us with a heavy, and perilous overthrow. At length we arrived at Bayeux, where we dined, at the house of a friend of my fair fellow traveller, to which she invited me with a tone of welcome, and good wishes, which overpowered all resistance. We sat down to an excellent dinner, at which was produced the usual favourite french dish of cold turbot, and raw artichokes. After our repast, a fine young woman, the daughter of the lady of the house, in a very obliging, but rather grave manner, poured out a tumbler full of some delicious potent liqueur, which, to my no small surprise, she presented me with; upon my only tasting it, and returning it, she appeared to be equally surprised, and confused. Her mother, observing our mutual embarrassment, informed me, that in France it was understood that the english were troubled with the ennui, or tristesse de cœur, and that they drank large draughts of wine and spirits to expel the gloomy malady. I softened this opinion of our common character, as well as I could, for, I fear, without offering considerable outrage to truth, I could not wholly have denied it.

After dinner, we walked to the cathedral, which is a noble gothic pile, and, upon our return, found the diligence in waiting for us. My companions were attended to the door of the carriage by their hospitable friends, between whom several kisses were interchanged. I took an opportunity, just before I mounted the step, of stealing one of these tokens of regard from the fair young damsel who had so courteously offered me the liqueur, at the same time telling her, that in England, a kiss was always considered as the best remedy for the tristesse de cœur.—Away trotted our little norman steeds; and, notwithstanding they had come all the way from Caen, they soon carried us over the hills on this side of Bayeux. The eye communicated delight to the heart, whilst it contemplated the vast extent of corn fields, which in this fertile province undulated on all sides of us, in waves of yellow exuberance, over which, embosomed in trees, at short distances, peeped the peaceful and picturesque abode of the prosperous cottage farmer. The prospect afforded an impressive contrast to the impolitic agricultural system, which has lately obtained in England, by which cottage farms are consolidated into ample domains of monopoly, and a baneful preference is given in favour of the rearing of cattle, to the vital and bountiful labours of the plough. A celebrated writer, who well knew in what the real wealth of a nation consisted, has observed, that he who could make two ears of corn grow upon a spot of ground, where only one grew before, would deserve better of mankind than the whole race of politicians. The high roads of Normandy are unnecessarily broad; hence considerable portions of land remain uncultivated. A spacious road, like every thing which is vast, excites an impression of grandeur; but in this prolific department, the facilities of travelling, and the dignity of the country, might be consulted with less waste. This prodigality is perhaps attributable to the highways in France having shared but little of its legislative attention; and accommodation appears to have been sought rather by a lavish allotment of space, than by a judicious formation, and frequent repair.

The inns along the road are very poor, although over the door of almost every little cottage is written, in large characters, "Bon Cidre de Victoire." There are also no regular post-horses to be met with. The country, on all sides of us, was very mountainous and luxuriant, and much resembled the southern parts of Devonshire. About seven o'clock in the evening of the same day, we arrived at St. Lo, which is, without exception, the cleanest and most charming, romantic little town, I saw in France. It is fortified, and stands upon the top of a mountain, at whose base is expanded a luxuriant scenery of woods and villages, through which the riviere de Ville winds in beautiful meanders. The inhabitants of this town appeared to be rich and genteel. In the evening I supped at the table d'hôte, where there were several pleasant people. At this town we slept, and set off, the next morning, very early, for Valogne, where we dined; and in the evening, after passing a considerable extent of rich meadow land, and descending a very steep hill, the freshness of the sea air announced to us our near approach to Cherbourg, where, at the hôtel d'Angleterre, I was soon afterwards landed. For my place and luggage to this place I paid twenty-four livres. My expenses upon the road were very reasonable. Here I had the good fortune to find a packet which intended to sail to England in two days, the master of which asked me only one guinea for my passage in the cabin, provisions included. However, thinking that the kitchen of a french vessel might, if possible, be more uncleanly than the kitchen of a french inn, I resolved upon providing my own refreshments for the little voyage.

Cherbourg

Cherbourg is a poor and dirty town. After having heard so much of its costly works and fortifications for the protection of its harbour, my surprise was not little, upon finding the place so miserable. It is defended by three great forts, which are erected upon rocks in the sea. The centre one is about three miles off from shore, and is garrisoned by 1200 men. At a distance, this fort looks like a vast floating battery. Upon a line with it, but divided by a distance sufficient for the admission of shipping, commences the celebrated, stupendous wall, which has been erected since the failure of the cones. It is just visible at low water. This surprising work is six miles in length, and three hundred french feet in breadth, and is composed of massy stones and masonry, which have been sunk for the purpose, and which are now cemented, by sea weed, their own weight and cohesion, into one immense mass of rock. Upon this wall a chain of forts is intended to be erected, as soon as the finances of government will admit of it. The expenses which have already been incurred, in constructing this wonderful fabric, have, it is said, exceeded two millions sterling. These costly protective barriers can only be considered as so many monuments, erected by the french to the superior genius and prowess of the british navy.

Whilst I was waiting for the packet's sailing, I received great civilities from Mons. C— —, the banker and american consul at Cherbourg, to whom I had letters from Mons. R— —. I rode, the second evening after my arrival, to his country house, which was about nine miles from the town. Our road to it lay over a prolific and mountainous country. From a high point of land, as we passed along, we saw the islands of Guernsey, Jersey and Alderney, which made a beautiful appearance upon the sea. Upon our return, by another road, I was much pleased with a group of little cottages, which were embosomed in a beautiful wood, through which there was an opening to the sea, which the sinking sun had then overspread with the richest lustre. As we entered this scene of rustic repose, the angelus bell of the little village church rang; and a short time afterwards, as we approached it, a number of villagers came out from the porch, with their mass-books in their hands, their countenances beaming with happiness and illuminated by the sinking sun, which shone full upon them. The charms of this simple scene arrested our progress for a short time. Under some spreading limes, upon a sloping lawn, the cheerful cottagers closed the evening with dancing to the sounds of one of the sweetest flagelets I ever heard, which was alternately played by several performers, who relieved each other. In France, every man is a musician. Goldsmith's charming picture of his Auburn, in its happier times, recurred to me:—

"When toil remitting, lends its turn to play,
And all the village train, from labour free,
Led up their sports beneath the spreading tree."

The cross roads of France are very bad; but, to my surprise, although we never could have had a worse specimen of them than what this excursion presented to us, yet the norman hunter upon which I was mounted, carried me over the deepest ruts, and abrupt hillocks, without showing the least symptom of infirmity which so much prevails amongst his brethren of the Devonshire breed. The norman horses are remarkable for lifting their feet high, and the safety and ease with which they carry their riders. In the morning of the day in which the packet was to sail, a favourable breeze sprung up; and, after undergoing the usual search of the revenue officers, in the execution of which they behaved with much civility, I embarked, and bade adieu to continental ground. The vessel had the appearance of being freighted with hot bread, with which the deck was covered from one end to the other. This immense collection of smoking loaves was intended for the supply of six men, and one woman, during a passage which we expected to accomplish in thirty hours, or less!

The faithful associate of our young captain, to whom she had just been married, either from motives of fondness or distrust, resolved upon sharing with him the perils of the ocean.

The sea-sufferings of this constant creature, and the resignation with which she endured them, sufficiently manifested the strength of her affections; for she was obliged to keep below all the time, and could afford but very little assistance in reducing the prodigious depot of bread which we had on board.

Credulous mariners describe a species of the fair sex (I believe the only one) who appear to much advantage upon the briny wave; but the nature of our commander's lady not happening to be amphibious, she gave such unequivocal proofs of being out of her proper element, that my wishes for shore increased upon me every minute.

During our passage, I could not help contrasting the habits of the english with the french sailors. The british tar thinks his allowance of salt beef scarcely digestible without a copious libation of ardent spirits, whilst the gallic mariner is satisfied with a little meagre soup, an immoderate share of bread, and a beverage of water, poor cider, or spiritless wine.

At length, after a passage of a day and a night, in which we experienced the vicissitudes of a stiff breeze, and a dead calm, we beheld

— —"That pale, that white-fac'd shore,
Whose foot spurns back the ocean's roaring tides,

And coops from other lands her islanders,
That water-walled bulwark, still secure
And confident from foreign purposes."

After passing another tedious night on board, owing to our being becalmed within the Needles, I stepped upon the same landing stone from which I first embarked for a country, where, in the centre of proscriptions, instability and desolation, those arts which are said to flourish only in the regions of repose, have, by their vigour and unrivalled bloom, excited the wonder and admiration of surrounding nations; where Peace, by her sudden and cherished reappearance, is calling forth all the virtues from their hiding places, to aid in effacing the corroding stains of a barbarous revolution, and in restoring the moral and social character to its pristine polish, rank and estimation.

GENERAL REMARKS.

The fact seems at first singular. Two of the greatest nations under Heaven, whose shores almost touch, and, if ancient tales be true, were once unsevered, call the natives of each other foreigners.

Jealousy, competition, and consequent warfare, have, for ages, produced an artificial distance and separation, much wider, and more impassable, than nature ever intended, by the division which she has framed; hence, whilst the unassisted eye of the islander can, from his own shores, with "unwet feet," behold the natural barrier of his continental neighbour, he knows but little more of his real character and habits, than of those of beings, who are more distantly removed from him, by many degrees of the great circle.

The events which have happened in France for the last eleven years, have rendered this separation more severe, and during that long and gloomy interval, have wholly changed the national character. Those who once occupied the higher class in the ascending scale of society, and who have survived the revolution without leaving their country, are no longer able to display the taste and munificence which once distinguished them. In the capital, those who formerly were accustomed to have their court yards nightly filled with carriages, and their staircases lined with lacqueys, are now scarcely able to occupy one third of their noble abodes. They cannot even enjoy the common observances of friendship, and hospitality, without pausing, and resorting to calculation. A new race of beings called the "nouveaux enrichés," whose services have been chiefly auxiliary to the war, at present absorb the visible wealth of the nation. Amongst them are many respectable persons. The lower orders of the people have been taught, by restless visionaries, to consider the destinations of Providence, which had before, by an imperceptible gradation of social colouring, united the russet brown to the magisterial purple, as usurpations over those natural rights which have been impressed without illustration, and magnified by a mischievous mystery. In the fierce pursuit of these imaginary immunities, which they had been taught to believe had been long withheld, they abruptly renounced all deference and decorum, as perilous indications of the fallacy of their indefinable pretensions, and were not a little encouraged by the disastrous desertion of their superiors, who fled at the first alarm. In short, the revolution has, in general, made the higher orders poor, and dispirited, and the lower barbarous, and insolent, whilst a third class has sprung up, with the silence and suddenness of an exhalation, higher than both, without participating in the original character of either, in which the principles of computation, and the vanity of wealth, are at awkward variance.

Until lately, the ancient french and the modern french were antipodes, but they are now converging, under a government, which, in point of security, and even of mildness, has no resemblance, since the first departure from the ancient establishments. The french, like the libertine son, after having plunged in riot and excesses, subdued by wretchedness, are returning to order and civilization. Unhappy people, their tears have almost washed away their offences—they have suffered to their heart's core. Who will not pity them to see their change, and hear their tales of misery? Yet, strange to relate, in the midst of their sighs and sufferings, they recount, with enthusiasm, the exploits of those very men, whose heroic ambition has trampled upon their best hopes, and proudest prosperity. Dazzled by the brilliancy of the spreading flame, they forget that their own abode is involved in its desolation, and augments the gloomy grandeur of the scene. To this cause may, perhaps, be traced that singular union of grief and gayety, which affords rather an impressive contrast to the more solemn consistency of english sadness. The terrible experiment which they have tried, has, throughout, presented a ferocious contest for power, which has only served to deteriorate their condition, sap their vigour, and render them too feeble either to continue the contest, or to reach the frontier of their former character. In this condition they have been found by a man who, with the precedent of history in one hand, and the sabre in the other, has, unstained with the crimes of Cromwell, possessed himself of the sovereignty; and, like Augustus, without the propensities which shaded his early life, preserved the *name* of a republic, whilst he well knows that a decisive and irresistible authority can alone reunite a people so vast and distracted; who, in the pursuit of a fatal phantom, have been inured to change, and long alienated from subordination. I would not wish such a government to be perpetual, but if it be conducted with wisdom and justice, I will not hesitate to declare, that I think it will ultimately prove as favourable to the happiness, as it has been propitious to the glory of the french. A government which breathes a martial spirit under a thin appearance of civil polity, presents but a barren subject to the consideration of the inquirer. When the sabre is changed into the sceptre, the science of legislation is short, simple, and decisive. Its energies are neither entangled in abstract distinctions, nor much impeded by the accustomed delays of deliberation.

From the magnitude of the present ruling establishment in France, and the judicious distribution of its powers, and confidence, the physical strength can scarcely be said to reside in the *governed*.

A great portion of the population participates in the character of the government. The bayonet is perpetually flashing before the eye. The remark may appear a little ludicrous, but in the capital almost every man who is not *near sighted* is a soldier, and every soldier of the republic considers himself as a subordinate minister of state. In short the whole political fabric is a refined system of knight's service. Seven centuries are rolled back, and from the gloom of time behold the crested spirit of the norman hero advance, "with beaver up," and nod his sable plumes, in grim approval of the novel, gay, and gaudy feodality.

If such an expectation may be entertained, that time will replace the ancient family on the throne, I am far from believing that it can offer much consolation to the illustrious wanderer, who as yet, has only tasted of the name of sovereignty. If the old royalty is ever restored, it is my opinion, and I offer it with becoming deference, that, from personal hatred to the present titular monarch, and the dread of retaliation by a lineal revival of monarchy, the crown will be placed upon the brows of one of the *collateral* branches of the expatriated family. The prince de Condé is the only member of that august house, of whom the french speak with esteem, and approbation.

The treasury of the french is, as may be expected, not overflowing, but its resources must speedily become ample. The necessities of the state, or rather the peculations of its former factious leaders, addressed themselves immediately to the purses of the people, by a summary process completely predatory. Circuitous exaction has been, till lately, long discarded. The present rulers have not yet had sufficient time to digest, and perfect a financial system, by which the establishments of the country may be supported by indirect, and unoffending taxation. Wisdom and genius must long, and ardently labour, before the ruins, and rubbish of the revolution can be removed. Every effort hitherto made to raise the deciduous credit of the republic has been masterly, and forcibly bespeaks the public hope, and confidence in favour of every future measure.

The armies of the republic are immense; they have hitherto been paid, and maintained by the countries which they have subdued; their exigencies, unless they are employed, will in future form an embarrassing subject of consideration in the approaching system of finance. This mighty body of men, who are very moderately paid, are united by the remembrance of their glory, and the proud consideration that they constitute a powerful part of the government; an impression which every french soldier cherishes. They also derive some pride, even from their discipline: a military delinquent is not subject to ignoble punishment; if he offend, he suffers as a soldier. Imprisonment, or death, alone displaces him from the ranks. He is not cut down fainting, and covered with the ignominious wounds of the dissecting scourge, and sent to languish in the reeking wards of hospitals.

In reviewing the present condition of France, the liberal mind will contemplate many events with pleasure, and will suspend its final judgment, until wisdom, and genius shall repose from their labours, and shall proclaim to the people, "behold the work is done."

It has been observed, that in reviewing the late war, two of the precepts of the celebrated author of "The Prince," will hereafter be enshrined in the judgments of politicians, and will be as closely adhered to, as they have been boldly disregarded by that great man, who, till lately, has long presided over the british councils. Machiavel has asserted, that no country ought to declare war with a nation which, at the time, is in a state of internal commotion; and that, in the prosecution of a war, the refugees of a belligerent power ought not to be confidentially trusted by the opposite nation which receives them. Upon violating the former, those heterogeneous parties, which, if left to themselves, will always embarrass the operations of their government, become united by a common cause; and by offending against the latter clause of this cautionary code, a perilous confidence is placed in the triumph of gratitude, and private pique, over that great love which nature plants and warmly cherishes in the breast of every man, for his country. In extenuation of a departure from these political maxims it may be urged, that the french excited the war, and that in the pursuit of it, they displayed a *compound* spirit, which Machiavel might well think problematical, for whilst that country never averted its eye from the common enemy, it never ceased to groan under the inflictions of unremitting factions. Rather less can be said in palliation of the fatal confidence, which was placed by the english government in some of the french emigrants. I have mentioned these unhappy people in the aggregate, with the respect which I think they deserve. To be protected, and not to betray, was all that could in fairness, and with safety be expected from them; it was hazarding too much to put swords in their hands, and send them to their own shores to plunge them in the breasts of their own countrymen: in such an enterprise

—————"The native hue of resolution
Is sicklied o'er with the pale cast of thought."

The brave have not frequently wept over such a victim as Sombrieul.

Whether the experiment of repelling those machinations which warred against all established order, and all sanctioned usage, by a novel, and unnatural opposition, is attributable to any other cause, than that of a misjudging principle, must be decided by Him, whose mighty hand suspended the balance of the battle, and whose eye can, at a glance, pierce through the labyrinth of human obliquity, however compact, shaded, or concealed. If the late minister is chargeable with a prolongation of the war, if he is responsible for having misplaced his confidence, and if brave men have perished by the fatal delusion, he will find some, if not ample consolation, in reflecting, that by his vigilance, and vigour, he has saved his country from the miseries of a revolutionary frenzy, which has rendered, even our enemies, the objects of our sympathy, and compassion.

Such is the narrowness of our nature, that we know not how adequately to appreciate our preservation from an *intercepted* evil: it is indistinctly seen, like a distant object. The calamity must *touch* before its powers and magnitude can be estimated. The flames of the neighbouring pile, must stop at our very doors, before our gratitude becomes animated with its highest energies. If Providence were to unfold to us all the horrours which we have escaped; if all the blood which would have followed the assassin's dagger were to roll in reeking streams before us; if the full display of irreligion, flight, massacre, confiscation, imprisonment and famine, which would have graced a revolutionary triumph in these realms, were to be unbarred to our view, how should we recoil from the ghastly spectacle! With what emotions of admiration and esteem should we bend before the man, whose illumined mind and dignified resolution protected us from such fell perdition, and confined the ravages of the "bellowing storm" within its own barrier.

The dazzling and perilous claims of the Rights of Man in the abstract, have had a long and ample discussion before the sanguinary tribunals of another country; and the loud decree of an indignant and insulted world has pronounced their eternal doom. Other contests may arise; but the powers of a prophet are not necessary to assert, that such rights will form no part of their provocation.

In France, I was repeatedly asked my opinion of the probable stability of the peace. The question was always addressed in this rather curious shape: "Thank God, we have peace! *Will your* country let us enjoy it?" — My answer was, "You may be assured of it; for it will not cease to be prepared for war."

Alas! the restless spirit of ambition seldom long delights in repose. The peaceful virtues, under whose influence Nations flourish and mankind rejoice, possess no lasting captivations for the Hero. The draught of conquest maddens his brain, and excites an insatiable thirst for fresh atchievements—He

"Looks into the clouds, scorning the base degrees
By which he did ascend" — —

May that extraordinary Being in whose hands the fate of millions is deposited reverse the gloomy picture, and restore to a country long wasted by revolutions, and warfare, and languishing in the midst of the monuments of her glory, the benign blessings of enduring tranquillity. But if this hope prove fruitless, if all the countries of continental Europe are destined to be compressed into one empire, if their devoted princes are doomed to adorn the triumphs of the chief of that mighty republic, which now towers above the surrounding nations of the earth, like the pyramid of the desert, what have we to fear even though the ocean which divides us should become the *soldiers* element?

When an enlightened frenchman is asked what he thinks of his government, his answer is, "We want repose." For this alone, a stranger to the recent occurrences of the world would think he had toiled, just as valetudinarians take exercise for the purpose of securing sleep. Even those who have profited of eleven years of desolation, are ready to acknowledge that war is not pastime, and that a familiarity with its horrours does not lessen them. The soldier, drooping under the weight of booty, pants for the refreshing shades of his native village, and for the hour which is to restore him to his alienated family.

I am satisfied, that both in France and England, one desire pervades all classes of people, that two nations, so brave, and so worthy of reciprocal esteem, may at last grow wise and virtuous enough to abstain from those ebullitions of furious hostility which have stained so many centuries with blood.

Peace is the gem with which Europe has embellished her fair but palpitating bosom; and may disappointment and dishonour be the lot of that ambitious and impolitic being who endeavours or who wishes to pluck it from her!

FINIS.

ERRATA.

For Lewis, read Louis.

For English, read own.

For import, read impost.

For bleu, read bleus.

For stories, read stones.

For entered now, read reentered.

For perpetual, read vast.

for profession, read will.

for the, read his.

for France, read the country.

for at, read of.

For hardworn, read hardwon.

Chap. XVIII, for Commodities, read Commodités.

For heightened, read high toned.

For is, read was.

Ult. after to, add those of.

For remblance, read resemblance.